'Cathy Burke reframes bus̶ leadership, and team-base̶ ̶ ̶a̶c̶h̶i̶e̶v̶ement. I have applied her work in three different companies across multiple cultures around the world, and this has made me a better senior leader and a more aligned complete person. These organisations, my teammates and the customers we have served have been the real beneficiaries of her unique insights.'

Steve Boehm
COO, Barings

'This book will cause you to swell into expansion and claim the mighty impact you're capable of. *Lead In* is Brené Brown meets Carol Dweck, and it's vital and magnificent.'

Emma Isaacs
CEO, Business Chicks

'If you want to succeed in any area the work always starts with yourself – not your competitors. Mindsets are the gateway to achievement and Cathy Burke is the globally recognised authority on how to make them work for you. Her insights and experience help organisations, entrepreneurs and change-makers lead themselves into the future.'

Daniel Priestley
CEO, Dent Global

'As a woman CEO in tech, Cathy has helped me let go of old thinking that never allowed me to pause, learn, reflect and grow, as there was always the next goal. Now there is no more second guessing, hiding or holding back. Even if you are a bold, leading edge, creative leader this book will transform your every day and change the way you think.'

Janelle King
CEO, Omnium Technology

'Cathy has been instrumental in implementing a mindset change across my leadership team which has turned a legacy business into a future-focused, dynamic enterprise. This has been done in a highly collaborative way that has been fit for purpose.'

Nick Nairn
CEO, Stuart Alexanders

'Cathy is one of those rare leaders who genuinely makes you look at your world from a new perspective and irreversibly changes your thinking as a result. Her blend of kindness, compassion and a healthy dose of tough love gives you no option to duck from the challenges she serves up, but your life will be richer in every sense of the word as a result of the lessons learned.'

Cathie Reid AM
Co-founder, Icon Group and Epic Pharmacy Group

'Cathy's expertise on mindset and leadership leads to exceptional results. I trust Cathy because her success comes from making those she works with accountable, empowered and ready for their success. She has made me a better leader, father and friend.'

Joris Heeze
Director, Global Selling and EU Brand Owner Success, Amazon

'Cathy's voice is so relevant for business right now. She is a courageous and powerful leader who is real, consistent, and engenders trust. Rather than limiting ideas of business to a money making and greedy lens, she looks at how service, purpose and delivery can merge so that stakeholders win.'

Colin Tate AM
CEO, Conexus Financial

'Cathy helps organisations transcend the day-to-day and achieve extraordinary outcomes.'

Ian Carson AM
Former Chairman of Markets, PwC
Executive Chair, Tanarra Capital

'I first met Cathy when I was looking to develop and open my teams' mindsets and grow their leadership capabilities. Smart, kind, and brilliant, Cathy knows her stuff. She creates the space for real, heartfelt sustainable change to happen – the type of change that is good for you, good for business and equips you for the challenges you face.'

Tania Austin
Owner and CEO, Decjuba

'I credit Cathy's advice, experience and workshops in my success in growing a non-profit globally across 100 countries reaching 10 million people.'

Scarlett Lewis
Founder and Chief Movement Officer,
Jesse Lewis Choose Love Movement

'Cathy is the kind of leader the world needs right now – down to earth, skilful and fearless - with bucket loads of integrity. She sees no 'other', just 'us'. She's always activating human goodness, whether it's empowering women around the world, transforming the mindsets of leaders, or mentoring agents of change. Cathy knows how to bring a vision into reality.'

Jono Fisher
Founder, Wake Up Sydney

'Whenever I listen to Cathy speak, or read her written work, she fills me with the determination to be a better me. Cathy has the unique ability to challenge us all to move beyond the blockages that are holding us back and to truly reach for our full potential.'

Dr David Cooke
Former Chair and Managing Director, Konica Minolta Australia
Chairperson, United Nations Global Compact, Australia
Director ESG Advisory

'Cathy has a unique ability to make a difference in any setting, whether it's a remote village in Ethiopia or the boardroom of a large company. Her understanding of people, leadership and change – and how she distils this and makes it relevant – is a rare gift.'

Alison Watkins
Director, Reserve Bank of Australia Board
Former Group Managing Director, Coca-Cola Amatil

'Cathy Burke is a trusted leader with a unique ability to recognize and unpack leadership attributes in all situations. She provides real world and relevant examples which make her leadership principles relevant and useful for teams and organisations.'

Barbi Buresh
Director, Global Voice of the Customer, eBay

'Cathy Burke has a brave heart and a brave head. She thinks about business as a force for good. Even when she leads from the front it always feels like support from the back. Her work in empowering women is flavoured with the kind of smarts, warmth and generosity particular to her.'

Karen Mahlab AM
Founder, Pro Bono Australia

'Cathy Burke has a unique ability to build rapport instantly with anyone, whether a villager in rural Bangladesh, or a board member in Sydney. Her ability to see though to the human in everyone makes her a truly gifted consultant and advisor in leadership and people development.'

Dr Joanna Martin
CEO and Founder, One of Many

'Cathy Burke has a very well-defined sense of social purpose and generosity of spirit. I trust her because she has shown results over time.'

David Gonski
Former Chair ANZ Banking Group
Chancellor of University of New South Wales

'Cathy's dedication and passion to help leaders to grow makes her an exceptional coach. She listened to our team's challenges and partnered with us to tackle opportunities together. She has helped my team think differently and guided us to find our own solutions.'

Hiromi Kuehn
Director, Regional Operations, Selling Partner Support, Amazon

'Cathy's ability to frame ideas into an executable action is why she stands out from other business leaders. The trust that Cathy's expressions convey is extremely potent.'

Steven Harker
Non-executive Director, Westpac Banking Group

'What I learned from Cathy motivated me to create programs for women which this year (2020) were recognized as "Diversity Initiative of the Year" by Women in IT.'

Trina Limpert
2020 President, Women@eBay
CEO, RizeNext Corp

Illuminating Sarah,

Thank you for your presence,
light e generosity of
spirit.

I'm so glad to have met you
at Nectar.

Lead In

♡ CM.

Lead In

Mindsets to Lead, Live
and Work Differently

CATHY BURKE

Published by Cathy Burke

First published in 2022 in Australia

Copyright © Cathy Burke

www.cathyburke.com

Back cover author photo by Millie Allbon

Edited by Jenny Magee

Typeset and printed in Australia by BookPOD

ISBN: 978-0-6453879-0-2 (paperback)
ISBN: 978-0-6453879-1-9 (ebook)

 A catalogue record for this book is available from the National Library of Australia

For Steven, Bronwen and Patrick

My loves, my lights and my lodestars.

Contents

Introduction   1

Chapter One: Why Mindsets Matter   11

Chapter Two: The Power of Mindset   25

Chapter Three: Four Mindsets   41

Chapter Four: The Leadership Quadrant   69

Chapter Five: The Leader's Mindset   95

Chapter Six: The Mindset Process   109

Chapter Seven: The Scarcity Mindset   153

Chapter Eight: Introducing the Mindset Process to Others   177

Afterword   193

Work with Cathy   197

About the Author   199

References   201

Introduction

Leadership is an inside job

But I didn't know that early on. Most people don't.

When I was new to work, it was all about the externals. Right from my first waitressing job, I worried about what others thought. 'Is the customer happy with how I took their order? Do I look ok? Will they blame me for the food taking too long?'

When I moved into office work, I'd worry what my colleagues thought. 'Do they think I'm incompetent? Should I say something, or will I sound stupid?' Later on, when working for a senator, I would be in a meeting and wonder whether I'd upset my boss. 'She's looking annoyed,' I'd worry. 'Is she happy with me? Did I do that right?'

Even when I started at The Hunger Project, the international NGO in which I became a global leader, while I was outwardly confident, I still worried about what others thought of me and whether I was

1

competent enough. I didn't want to let anyone down. Comments and feedback became gospel. For the first few years, I shaped my presence and reactions to fit what others thought and what was happening around me.

Leading this way unmoored me. In my naïvety and insecurity as a young and inexperienced CEO, I got too caught up in the throwaway comments of board members, or what business leaders thought of me, or how donors would react. Like a weathervane moving with the wind, I was 'leading out' – entirely reactive to whatever was happening externally.

This approach blunted my effectiveness. I was still passionate about the mission, but I was stuck. There was always another village to support and another partnership to hang my hopes on. I was like a dog chasing a car I could never catch, always questing outwards to find what I should do and who I should be. Leading out is exhausting and unsatisfying. Your attention is constantly on what's outside your control – what others think, how you appear to them, or some shiny new thing on the horizon.

In leading out, more fortunate times can only happen with a change in your circumstances – not from anything you do. When you get a better team, or the market settles down – then you will be successful and less stressed.

Most of the world runs this way, which is why the antidote, to *lead in*, is so rare. To *lead in* brings the power and responsibility back to you, no matter what difficulties are happening around you. Instead of placing your energy and attention on what you can't change, you use that energy to achieve your goals in ways that renew and ground you.

Leading in is the antithesis of unaware and ego-driven decision-making that stymies creativity, inclusion and breakthrough. It requires self-awareness – a fundamental skill that all great leaders learn. Such leaders question themselves, and their mindsets. They are curious: 'What are my motivations? What's most important here? What beliefs and assumptions do I hold about this?'

When we become aware of what's happening within us, we are far more effective at moulding and shaping what happens around us.

I've written *Lead In* to ground and equip you to make the changes that matter in your life and your world. Making these requires authenticity and courage. It's so much easier (initially) to play the same record over and over instead of finding your own groove. Yet when we become aware of what's happening within us, we are far more effective at moulding and shaping what happens around us. This is the essence and magic of *leading in*.

Bookstore shelves hold hundreds of books that insist we should be more or do more. 'Live Your Best Life!' 'Sell Yourself!' 'Change the World!' Of course, they sound amazing – full of stories of trailblazing CEOs, brilliant entrepreneurs and ordinary people transformed by life-changing practices.

These books tell us to 'back yourself', 'be vulnerable' and 'believe you can do it'. And while I love the idea of this, I'm never quite sure who they are talking to. I mean, I understand how Steve Jobs got to be so brilliant, but what about the average person? What about me? Whatever tips those books contain, it can be hard to know what to do with them.

That's because none of this wisdom is fully available while we focus outwards. You can only access it by getting under your own limiting beliefs and unexamined assumptions. You might agree with great truths because they make complete sense, but applying them? The same old story you've always heard whispers 'not you – you're not smart enough, or confident enough, or born with the right skills', and this trips you up in the cold light of day. Accessing great truths and wisdom without inner reflection and practice is like pouring water on sand and hoping a garden will grow. We keep searching outside for a solution that will fix our dissatisfaction on the inside. But we are looking in the wrong place.

I understand this dynamic, and I discovered for myself how working with mindsets is key to leading with grace and effectiveness. I stopped being reactive and diffusing my focus and energy. I came to know and heed my internal compass. Using mindsets to *lead in* increased my impact and my scope for joy.

But it wasn't always that way.

We are more than our past

Any worthwhile achievements in my life have come from powerful mindset shifts that refocused me from looking outside for approval or guidance towards mindful, creative and courageous leadership. That wasn't how it started.

I'm one of seven children from a family that struggled severely with finances and mental health. My father was unemployed for many years, so Mum did whatever she could to put food on the table. She made wantons for the local Chinese restaurant, worked the nightshift cleaning at a two-star hotel, bet on the horses, and typed the newsletter for the local Catholic Church. I grew up with the belief – and the lived proof – that life is unfair and money is hard to come by.

Mum also struggled with severe depression, and I hated it when the nuns at my school would ask with pity, 'And how is your mother?' Embarrassed and ashamed of the situation at home, I became an outsider, never quite fitting in. I didn't want people to get close in case they saw our family hardship. To add to this, I was hospitalised with severe asthma up to a dozen times a year. By the time I left high school, I was a very prickly person indeed.

I explain this because the ideas we form in childhood linger into adulthood. They can become the mindsets and beliefs that determine our decisions and even our identities. We each have our version. I was the sick one, the poor one and the distant one.

In early adulthood, exposure to different ways of thinking about the world interrupted this perspective. For the first time, I started to think about why I did things I did and what I wanted to achieve. It began when I looked for ways to cure my asthma, and while I didn't find that particular pot of gold, meditation and personal development programs helped me consider the role I played in my own life.

For the first time, I started to think about why I did things I did and what I wanted to achieve.

As my focus shifted away from outward excuses based on my childhood circumstances, I got the first inklings that I was not fated to live my life as it had always been. While I never heard the word 'mindset', it was the beginning of noticing and questioning old thought patterns and choosing new ways of being. This awakening had profound repercussions across so much of my life – including getting married (thirty plus years and still going strong!), becoming a parent, and eventually leading an organisation committed to ending hunger.

A leading mindset

The Hunger Project was my life-changing introduction to mindsets and their fundamental importance in accomplishing change. Typically, when we are mired in difficulties or facing hostile external conditions, we focus outwards, reacting to the situation and looking for ways to fix it. This might look like swinging into action – or anger – without thinking, when something unwanted happens to you. Or it might be telling yourself that things are too hard, that the circumstances are overwhelming, and giving up. Either way, you focus on the conditions and yourself relative to those conditions. Your power and agency are missing.

On the other hand, mindsets focus on what you can control. They are the ultimate tool for a *lead in* leader, and it was women and men in villages, overcoming decades of hunger and poverty, who showed me this.

I first became aware of The Hunger Project when working for a senator, who told me about its mission to end hunger. At the time, it seemed overwhelming. Could hunger even end? Weren't there more than a billion people to feed?

I put it to one side, but after the birth of my first child, The Hunger Project's bold mission to end hunger came into sharp focus for me. As

I held my newborn daughter, it seemed inconceivable that any parent could lose their child through starvation or a preventable illness like diarrhoea or the common cold – just because of the place where they were born.

I became passionate about the organisation's mission to empower people to end hunger, centring the hungry as the key players in all efforts. It spoke to me so powerfully – and still does.

The Hunger Project does not see hungry people as the problem – they are the solution. They are not an immovable mountain of need, waiting to be saved. Instead, they are hard-working, creative, courageous humans who do the lion's share of the work in ending hunger. This perspective stirred my soul. It spoke to the power of human possibility, offering a completely different mindset on who gets to lead and what they need to succeed.

When my daughter was a few months old, I became a volunteer and a financial contributor. I educated myself on the issues and mobilised others to get involved. Trips to Ethiopia and India connected me further to the cause and seared the complexity and scale of hunger onto my soul. I was committed to doing whatever I could to bring this to an end.

Joining The Hunger Project staff in 1997 increased my engagement, and was my trial by fire as a leader. It upended my 'small me' view of myself. Me, lead? Even with my old stories and limiting mindsets, time and again, I found the courage to step into my power.

In no small part, this was due to the incredible breakthroughs people were having in their communities. They faced enormous obstacles and every possible reason to fail. In villages where women were not listened to, they refused to fall back; they kept moving forward and drove immense change. Despite the odds, these women succeeded. They became my greatest teachers.

Over time I built a beloved and successful organisation that contributed significantly to global programs and strategies to help end hunger. I've sat on village floors the world over and spoken at some of the most prestigious international forums. I mobilised significant financial and human resources toward the mission of ending hunger. Every step challenged one limiting belief and old story that I held after another. There was no tumultuous breakthrough for my leadership, just an endless series of moments where I chose and rechose to *lead in*.

The promise of this book

This book melds the possible and the practical, unpacking ways to change our scripts of who we think we are. I've written it to be actionable and useful. At every stage in life and business, we face obstacles and barriers to what we want to achieve. This might be in your career where you're just not getting the results you want, or in your relationships that feel tired and strained. You might lead a team that is wrung out and exhausted, or you feel powerless at what is happening in the world. Instead of reacting and immediately focusing on fixes or blame, *Lead In* will be your guide to help you overcome and transform these barriers.

Chapters One, Two and Three unpack what leadership is and the role of mindsets. They explore how mindsets are foundational to work that inspires and impacts.

Chapter Four covers some default leading styles and makes the case that these are not who you are.

Chapter Five homes in on the ultimate *lead in* tool – the Leader's mindset.

Chapter Six turns the spotlight on you and takes you through the Mindset Process – a four-part approach to identifying and changing mindsets that are holding you back. Get your pen and paper ready, you'll be getting to work!

Chapter Seven examines one of the most widespread limiting mindsets that most people share. It's not quite the mindset that rules them all – but almost!

And finally, in Chapter Eight, you'll learn how to share the Mindset Process to develop more leaders in your life and your organisation who also *lead in*.

Lead In offers ideas around leadership and inclusion that are essential for tackling twenty-first-century challenges. I hope that this book will liberate more engaged and conscious leadership in all walks of life. Given the enormity of the issues at hand, reacting from fear and old patterns doesn't cut it anymore. Second-guessing ourselves, not believing we are good enough, and ignoring the stress and tension in our organisations are all inhibitors to moving forward.

This book will help you identify and move on from old limiting stories and mindsets to a new way of leading, living and working that represents you at your most expansive. You will find a way to inhabit the world more freely. You will understand that you have more ability than you know and that the world is eager to meet you where you are. You will realise that you have what it takes to make your contribution.

One

Why Mindsets Matter

Challenging our beliefs

In early 1998 I attended a week-long meeting at The Hunger Project global headquarters in New York City. The organisation's president, Joan Holmes, outlined a new strategy to put women at the centre of all its programs. It was ground-breaking stuff.[1]

The United Nations' Fourth World Conference On Women in 1995 had marked a turning point in the global agenda and alignment for gender equality. It spelled out clearly that 'Women's poverty is directly related to the absence of economic opportunities and autonomy, lack of access to economic resources, lack of access to education and support services, and their minimal participation in the decision-making process.'[2] This understanding became a global clarion call.

Even though The Hunger Project already had successful development initiatives, Holmes was clear that none of these would continue without a radical redirection that put women at the centre of programs and decision-making. The urgent need to empower women could not be denied.

I was inspired and swept up. Holmes' stand catalysed a massive mindset shift for the organisation – and for me. Throughout many days of meetings, I wrote copious notes on why it was vital for women's voices to be heard. On page after page, I was on fire with what it would mean to empower the leadership of women living with hunger. Elevating their voices would enable them to influence decisions in their households and villages. It was (and is) amazing and radical, and I was on board.

During the meeting, I got a tap on the shoulder by executive vice president, Dr John Coonrod, inviting me outside for a private discussion. John said The Hunger Project needed a country director or CEO in Australia, and he believed I should be that person.

I was flummoxed. Me? CEO? I was a passionate staffer, hugely committed to the organisation and mission, but I had never led anything like that before. So I said no. I fobbed his offer off with some nonsense along the lines of, 'I don't think we need a CEO. That's just not the way we do things in Australia. We're more egalitarian…' (I still cringe to remember this!). Coonrod said, 'Ok, that's disappointing', and we went back to the session with Joan Holmes.

Moments later, the penny dropped when looking at my notes on how *those women* needed to find their voice and power to lead their communities. There were no *those women*. There were just *women*! I, too, was caught up in old ideas of what leadership looked like and who got to wield it. Without any consideration, I had just cut myself off from a position that would increase my impact. I came face-to-face with my unexamined mindsets about myself as a leader – too young, not experienced enough, not from the right background.

History shows that I did accept the invitation to lead as the Australia CEO. Still, I am struck by how close it came to not happening and how easy it was to pass that invitation up, based on nothing other than a limited view of what leadership is and who leaders really are.

To *lead in*

This book is about how to lead differently – but what does leading even mean? This is an essential question because creating a conscious and empowered relationship to leadership is vital for our world, our communities and our organisations to thrive.

Too often, leadership is seen as a role conferred upon someone, like a job title or a crown. That is true in some cases – but it doesn't tell the whole story. Like me, you might be offered an opportunity to lead, but you hesitate because you think it isn't you. We see people clearly unsuited to leadership roles and wonder how they got there. Or we see leaders who all look and talk the same way – and it's not a way we connect with. However we view it, leadership has the smell of a dark art about it. It's either a boys' club or full of people who claw and backstab their way to get it. No wonder many amazing people look at leading and say 'no thanks'.

We must reimagine leadership
and place ourselves within
that reimagination.

Leadership cannot remain the prized possession of a few. We must dismantle old ideas about leadership and power and reclaim the word and its legitimacy. We must reimagine leadership and place ourselves within that reimagination.

Rather than a dark art, or the domain of 'male, pale and stale', the leadership I believe in is brighter, more alive and quite different. Simply put, a leader is someone who takes action to impact an area that's meaningful to them. They reimagine a future as better and work to bring that about. This leader does not need followers. They require no passing of the mantle, or a corner office. They are found in kitchens, in schools, in homes, in hallways, in neighbourhood centres, on buses, at the post office, online, in villages, on farms, in skyscrapers – and yes (sometimes), even in corner offices! This idea of leadership is inclusive and available. It speaks the truth about our potential to make a difference. We don't need to be anointed, we just need to *lead in*.

To *lead in* means two things; to lead within yourself and be aware of what is going on for you. What is important to you? What beliefs are you holding? How do you choose to behave? How will you show up? It also means leading in our organisations, communities, and world. We need more people to lead in their sphere of influence with personal awareness, courage and heart – and then extend this into the world to help make life better.

To *lead in* demands an inner reckoning with your personal power and agency. Only you can claim authority for your vision and your life. To do this means focusing less on the small questions that often emphasise the non-essentials, such as 'What do they think of me? How do I get them to like me? Who's at fault? How do I get what's mine?'

Our world encourages us to obsess about these smaller questions, yet devoting our life to them is unfulfilling. As the mythologist Joseph

Campbell wrote, 'there is perhaps nothing worse than reaching the top of the ladder and discovering that you're on the wrong wall.'

Leading in requires us to ask and answer bigger questions.

Leading in requires us to ask and answer bigger questions: 'What really matters to me? How can I contribute to the greater good? What is the courageous action I could take? What impact do I want to make? What could be possible were I to stop playing small? What is the calling of my own heart?'

A *lead in* leader goes beyond what they are told is important. They focus on who they are in the matter of their own life – not in relation to others' expectations. They find their internal compass and take action from there.

What is leadership?

In 1993 in Ouagadougou, Burkina Faso, Joan Holmes gave a description of leadership that resonates to this day. At the announcement for the Africa Prize for Leadership for the Sustainable End of Hunger, she defined leaders as 'individuals who work at the frontier where tomorrow is taking shape'. She continued: 'The key to leadership is responsibility. A leader must say to him or herself that, "even though I have inherited this problem – a problem that I did not cause – this problem is now mine. With your participation, I will solve it."'[3]

These words still have the force of truth for me, nearly thirty years on.

I love that with this definition of leadership, Holmes invites us all to participate in solving challenges. She removes it from the usual right/wrong paradigm that derails meaningful action. How often do we lose steam because we get bogged down in blame or looking for reasons why a problem exists? Holmes' perspective rises above this. She is committed to galvanising the energy and ownership of many people to find a solution rather than narrowing it into apportioning blame. She asks us to see ourselves and our actions as the 'frontier where tomorrow is taking shape'. Imagine empowering the people in your team or your community that way. What frontier do you want to work in? This is the territory of a *lead in* leader.

Brené Brown's definition also describes this new leadership paradigm as one of responsibility and impact. In *Dare To Lead*,[4] she writes that a leader is 'anyone who takes responsibility for finding the potential in people and processes, and who has the courage to develop that potential'.

It's no accident that Brown, like Holmes, talks about leadership as a responsibility. When we take this up and step into our power to make a difference – in our own lives or the larger world – responsibility comes with it. Perhaps some people shy away from leading because they see responsibility as a burden. But when leadership is fully chosen, it is liberating. When you choose to *lead in*, you step up. You influence. You determine what's important to you. You get to have a say about what you want to cause – in your organisation, your family, and your world. You truly get to create your life.

Our biggest obstacle

In thinking about the life you want, you'll find many things get in the way. Sometimes you can move around them, but at other times they'll stop you in your tracks. They become the reason why you can't achieve your aims. You believe that if only that obstacle was removed, then you would be happy and achieve more.

This book will ask you to consider that the biggest obstacle to making changes and getting amazing stuff done is not the circumstances – even when they really suck. What's getting in the way is not your boss. It's not your annoying colleague or ungrateful client. It's not your weight. It's not even a pandemic.

That might surprise you. Surely the things that happen to you outside your control are the biggest obstacles to achieving your goals? That makes sense, but no.

Your biggest obstacle is your mindset.

Your mindset limits or expands your field of accomplishment and impact – especially when you can't change the circumstances. With the right mindset, you can shift your thinking and match your beliefs with inspired action. Changing even a single belief that has held you back will see your life improve in positive and powerful ways.

Your biggest obstacle is your mindset.

Mindsets can seem incongruent because our culture trains us to look outside ourselves for the source of our problems. When you're under pressure, it seems logical to deal with whatever is causing stress. Yet perhaps surprisingly, when the issue is complex, this is not an effective first step. Of course, if you have a hole in your boat, then fix the hole, but most of our challenges aren't that simple. You can spend lots of effort attacking a problem, but unless you address the underlying mindset, it's like cutting the head off a hydra – another problem will raise its head.

In *The 7 Habits of Highly Effective People*,[5] the late Dr Stephen Covey wrote that working hard is ineffective if we are not 'sharpening the saw'. Labouring away, inefficiently expending energy is not smart. We must take time to ensure our tools are in the best shape possible, and mindsets are some of the finest in our toolkit.

What gets in your way

If you're reading this, you likely have big dreams, unfulfilled yearnings, or goals you want to achieve. You might be a corporate executive running a large team that serves thousands of customers. Perhaps you are at a new stage in life and want to create something more aligned with who you are now. You might be new to leadership and want to do the best job possible. Or you are a business owner employing good people. You might be newly returned to the workforce after extended leave. Or an activist passionate about making a meaningful impact.

We all get stuck sometimes and get in our own way. We start to second-guess ourselves, and doubt and frustration win out over hope and achievement. In an instant, the space we have to move in shrinks. One moment we're feeling good about life, then something happens – it might be as minor as a friend's post on Instagram – and boom! We head into a downward spiral of comparison, judging how little we've done with our lives.

When this happens, we try to compensate. We might try to suppress the discomfort with behaviours we know will soothe – at least temporarily. Out come the biscuits, the chocolate, the wine, and on goes Netflix and online shopping.

We admonish, shame, or trash-talk ourselves. 'I'm an idiot.' 'Why did I say that?' 'I shouldn't have done that.' 'I'll never make it.' We ruminate and get stuck in endless mental loops.

Or we look externally to try and solve our problems. We think, 'Well, if only that hadn't happened, then I'd be ok,' or 'I'll never make that goal because the competition was rigged from the start'. In doing so, we hand over our power. We get stuck looking for an external source to solve our problem.

While we love it when the cards fall in our favour, it is a childish strategy for happiness and fulfilment. Life does what life does. Ranting or waiting for things to change is not leadership. Instead, developing mindset skills is key to getting back on track.

Mindset work is necessary for any real, lasting and meaningful change. It isn't a luxury set aside for people with time and money. Nor is it shirking the real challenges we face – as a species and as individuals.

Mindset work is necessary for any real, lasting and meaningful change.

Mindset work is an essential tool to solving huge issues. It gives us access to power – especially when external conditions are unfair and overwhelming. I observed this firsthand from women and men living in hunger across Africa and South Asia. From them, I learned how humans can rise, and the power of activating a leader's mindset.

Mindsets? Really?

Few of us can imagine the depth and entrenchment of the issues and challenges people face in communities with hunger. They are, in any estimation, overwhelming and seemingly insurmountable. I've spent time with people who had sick children and no access to a doctor; farmers who had little food and no rain to grow the crops in the ground; girls, married too young, who became mothers too soon. These conditions that so many of our human family endure are unfair and unjust.

At the beginning of this work, whether in Senegal or India, Ethiopia or Bangladesh, I thought I understood the reasons for hunger – and how it could be fixed. I could always point my finger at something external: social and educational structures that bypass the poor; patriarchal beliefs that subjugate women and girls; climate change that exacerbates the water issues facing small scale farmers; legacies of colonialism that keep people mired in poverty; endemic corruption that took money from the poor and gave it to the rich. Surely these were the reasons for hunger and poverty. And yes, these are all true. However, with only this context, the source of hunger seemed to sit outside of people affected – as did the solution to ending it.

When I first heard about mindset and its role in ending hunger, I felt uncomfortable. How on earth could mindset address entrenched systemic subjugation? Attributing the problems to the people felt like victim-blaming. It was understandable that the people most affected by hunger would feel overwhelmed and powerless. Many shared that they thought God had deserted them or that they could do nothing. They believed the only thing that could change their situation would be help from outside – or a miracle. But their decades of lived experience suggested neither was likely to happen, so despair prevailed. It all made complete sense. Anyone in that situation would feel the same way.

So you might understand why the emphasis on mindsets made me feel uneasy. But this reaction was mainly because I didn't understand what they were. Like many people, I confused mindsets with positive thinking, or affirmations, or even mindfulness. Perhaps you do too. I felt that this focus on mindsets denied the reality of people's lives and minimised the challenges they woke up to every day. It seemed to pass judgement on people who were already suffering hugely.

Like many people, I confused mindsets with positive thinking, or affirmations, or even mindfulness.

I couldn't have been more wrong.

Working with mindsets is foundational to transformative change and the source of bold, breakthrough leadership. This doesn't take away the need for urgent structural reform, equity, and economic justice. Large scale global initiatives are needed. The United Nations Sustainable Development Goals are an example of the concerted and coordinated effort required to confront and overcome systemic inequities.[6] Yet, a singular focus on global mechanisms locks out the power of the people themselves. Unlocking this power is critical to sustainable solutions, and mindsets hold the key.

As we will see, mindsets have the power to restore a human being to their deepest agency – their ability to choose for themselves what they think and believe and then match this with action.

Our beliefs keep us small

Empowering people to understand their mindsets gives them the tools to rethink assumptions of power and their relationship to it. It embraces the potential of humans to light a torch within that allows for transformation.

Humans are conditioned to believe that our problems are rooted in what happens outside of us – in the externalities and the circumstances – and thus can only be solved from there. As a result, in every challenge facing humanity, we overlook the true source of power – the power of the human spirit – and a person's ability to lead, create and transform.

This is equally true in an organisation as it is in a village. Without even realising it, we all get locked into beliefs and assumptions about the world we live in, the people we work with, and our own limitations. These end up defining what we do and don't do. As a result, we hobble our ability to change the narrative and the prevailing view. It keeps us small.

If you constrain and diminish your space in the world because you say you are too shy to have your opinion heard, too old to make a difference, or too fearful of making much-needed changes, then look no further than your mindset.

If you believe you are not 'leadership material' because of the way you look and dress or the work you do and the position you hold, consider your mindset.

If you think 'I've always been this way and can't change', or 'it won't work, we tried it before', then look closer at which mindsets are at play.

I have seen real-world change in countless villages and communities when people activate their mindsets and *lead in*. I've also seen this in the world's largest companies, small businesses, schools, not-for-profit organisations and families. It is foundational to our human ability to change the world. If we fail to *lead in*, we will always be at the mercy of what is done to and around us, and we will never be free. We will be doomed to impotency – shaking our fists at the vagaries of fate.

It needn't be this way.

Key points

- Your greatest avenue to achieving success and making something extraordinary happen does not lie in your circumstances lining up. It lies in your mindset.

- You *lead in* yourself, your organisation, family, community, and world.

- Developing a leader's mindset does not need anyone's permission. It doesn't require a job title. It does, however, require you to own your ability to make an impact on something important to you.

- You are never *too* anything to start living your dreams! You are not too young, too old, too junior, too different, too (fill in the gap) to achieve your goals.

Questions to consider

- What are your big dreams?
- What gets in the way of making them happen?

Two

The Power of Mindset

Current understanding around mindset burst into public awareness in large part through the research and thought leadership of Carol Dweck, professor of psychology at Stanford University. Dweck published a seminal book called *Mindset: The New Psychology of Success* in 2006,[7] based on decades of research that began with how children learn in schools and expanded to include an understanding of human motivation across all ages.

Mindsets are the stories, assumptions, and beliefs we tell ourselves about ourselves, others, the world, or our situation. Over time these beliefs can become our truth. We stop questioning or even seeing them. They become the background we don't notice; they are 'just the way it is', like the wall holding up the ceiling or the sky being blue. Mindsets become the platform we build our lives on, but we don't recognise how they determine what we build and how we live.

How mindsets are formed

Many of our most entrenched mindsets form in childhood. Even before we could speak, we made sense and meaning from our environment. We worked out how to get attention. We learned what our family valued. We absorbed ideas and concepts like a sponge, without the critical thinking ability to sift and filter what we learned.

According to Fiona Boylan from Edith Cowan University, most babies and toddlers start out 'willing to take a chance and to have a go at things. We don't tend to see in them that helplessness or the response of "I won't have a go, because I'm not sure if I can". Once children get to about three years of age, that starts to change. Their beliefs about their intelligence or learning abilities are influenced by the messages they receive from others about their abilities to do different tasks.'[8]

In each family and culture, certain qualities are valued over others. And even with parents' best intentions, kids get labelled. 'Jack is the funny one, and Jill is the kind one' might seem innocuous or even complimentary, but if said often enough can become part of one's identity and can limit other possible ways of showing up in the world. As an adult, Jack's go-to strategy becomes telling a joke, making it hard for his teammates to share their concerns. At the same time, Jill finds it challenging to have brave but uncomfortable conversations because she is locked into a view of herself as being kind.

Like labels, being praised only for your ability and not for how you did something or the effort that took, creates beliefs that limit us. Praise can be like a dopamine hit or a reward – Pavlov's dog style. When kids are lauded for their ability – 'you're a natural!' – they do more of what will get them appreciated and celebrated and less of what takes struggle and effort. Over time we start to believe only in our natural ability. Exertion and persistence for success are not seen as valid or desired.

Children don't develop logical and critical thinking until at least age eleven. The prefrontal cortex (that part of the brain that is our critical thinking and executive function) is not mature until after age twenty. Plenty of beliefs are formed and shaped before then, slipping through the mental net.

The good news is, we can develop more expansive and empowering mindsets. As Dweck says 'Mindsets are just beliefs. They're powerful beliefs, but they're just something in your mind, and you can change your mind.'[9] It takes time, but you can identify and change beliefs that don't serve you.

Stuck behind a mindset

Vanessa is a marketing whiz who felt stuck in her career. While what she had achieved was commendable, she was tired of living behind a keyboard, writing strategies and copy for products she wasn't interested in. Vanessa was thinking about changing her career and studying to be a psychologist. She was fascinated by human development and loved the idea of working to help others.

However, she was put off by the statistics component of the degree, so she had not submitted her application for the new intake. Vanessa felt lost. She wondered if she should just 'suck it up' with her current career, 'I mean, I like writing (I guess), and I'm good at it.' But this decision left her feeling flat.

This was Vanessa's mindset at play. She was cutting out the possibility of an exciting new career because she believed she was hopeless at maths. Using the Mindset Process we'll learn about in Chapter Six, Vanessa recalled enjoying numbers in primary school. 'It felt good to work the sums out. I didn't think I was good or bad – it was just fun, and I liked figuring out problems.'

Yet over time, Vanessa decided that she wasn't good at maths. There was no great moment or crisis. She said, 'Maybe I just absorbed the belief that girls weren't good at maths. But at some point, it felt that maths wasn't my thing, not like spelling and English, where I got good marks and praise. A story I wrote when I was twelve was so good it got published in the paper and people noticed. Writing kinda became my thing.'

Given both the praise and labelling she'd received for spelling and writing, it's no surprise Vanessa doubled down on that, even making it her career. Recognising that 'I'm no good at maths' was an old story – and not necessarily true – gave her the courage to leave a job that was no longer satisfying and embark on a new direction in line with what she wanted. Vanessa's concerns about statistics were still there, but she realised she could get the help she needed to be able to tackle that, without the old mindset as a blocker.

What have you given up on or not explored because of a decision you made long ago? Was it that you will never be good with money? That you aren't good at sport? These beliefs govern the choices we make about every aspect of life.

What have you given up on or not explored because of a decision you made long ago?

The research proves this. According to Dweck,[10] 'the view you adopt for yourself profoundly affects the way you lead your life. It can determine whether you become the person you want to be and whether you accomplish the things you value. How does this happen? How can a simple belief have the power to transform your psychology and, as a result, your life?'

How indeed.

How mindsets work

Mindsets are like glasses that we put on. Over time we forget we are even wearing them. Imagine you put on a pair of blue glasses. At first, the world seems blue. Everything you look at is blue, and after a while, you forget what it was like before you wore them. Over time, the world doesn't just look blue to you. It *is* blue.

Now imagine your work colleague is wearing a pair of red glasses. You just can't seem to get any alignment or agreement between you. That's because while it's true that the world is blue for you, for them, it is equally valid that the world is red. Without understanding the different lenses through which you both see the world, it's hard to find common ground. You just make each other wrong.

To complicate things even further, we don't just have one mindset. Over time we pick up and wear more and more pairs of glasses. We put on the 'I'm not good enough' glasses; the 'It didn't work before so it won't now' glasses, or the 'world's going to hell in a hand basket' glasses. One popular pair that many people wear is the 'I don't have enough' glasses. There are plenty more. Like a focusing lens, each mindset narrows the aperture through which you see the world, and over time your world gets smaller and smaller.

When we are unaware of our mindsets, we hand over our autonomy to them. Like a computer operating system, they tick away in the background, determining what we do (and don't do), what we say yes (or no) to, and even who (and if) we go into a relationship with.

As we have discovered, many limiting mindsets have been with us for as long as we can remember. Carefully honed over time, they feel like us, our personality. Who we are. We make decisions based on them. They feel real and true because we have history together! 'I can't go for that promotion, I'm not confident enough'. 'It's no use trying to learn French, I'm just not good with languages.' 'I'd like to be in a relationship, but all the good ones are taken.' See how real these feel? Perhaps you believe one of these too. Mindsets have a familiar, lived-in quality to them. They feel true. So much so, we never question them.

Given that mindsets are the stories, beliefs and identities we gather over time, we find lots of proof that they are right. It's a form of confirmation bias, where we favour and look for information that validates our experience and ignore or repudiate evidence that contradicts it.

When things matter

Mindsets are neither inherently good nor bad. It's more helpful to consider whether they are useful for your growth and aspirations, or not.

Gardening provides a great example. Issa has a mindset that she is no good with plants – and she has plenty of proof of that! She's not really interested in gardening, so she never weeds and forgets to water, and plants die. Therefore, she forms a belief that 'I don't have a green thumb', and never gardens.

Priyanka, however, has a mindset about gardening that is curious and enlivening. She coaxes plants along and loves learning about cultivation. She experiments with seedlings and cuttings. Some die, but that's ok! It prompts her to learn more about what a particular plant needs to thrive. Issa's mindset has her look at Priyanka's garden and think, 'Wow, you are so talented. I'll never be like that'. Issa sees Priyanka's success as an ability that is not available to her, rather than a skill she too can learn. With Issa's mindset, a skill (gardening) is something you either have or don't have – and she doesn't.

This is a minor example, but it shows how unexamined mindsets can determine what we do or don't do. The stakes here are small; whether your mindset is 'I'm bad with plants' or 'I'm good with plants' won't matter if you don't care about gardening. Mindsets become crucial around the stuff we're committed to – those essential things we want most in life.

Mindsets become crucial around the stuff we're committed to – those essential things we want most in life.

Mindsets that block meaningful pursuits may look innocuous, but they're not. You might have a business idea you are stalling on (it's not ready), a promotion you want to go for (I'm not confident enough), a book you are procrastinating writing (what if people think it's crap?), a team you need to lead (they'll find out I don't know what I'm doing). These mindsets limit, and sometimes downright sabotage, what we are committed to. They leave no scope for growth, change, or possibility. That is why, when they are left unchecked, we feel frustration, stress and pain.

If you're stuck in any area of your life, then consider that it's your mindset in the way, not a permanent lack in some natural and finite bag of skillsets.

Mindset for ending hunger

Mindsets aren't just valuable for freeing our narrow view of ourselves; they are also critical for solving complex problems.

Before returning to his country of Bangladesh, Badiul Majumdar was a professor of finance and economics at two prestigious American universities for twenty years. He was also a former student of Peter Drucker, the educator, economist and author often described as the founder of modern management. Majumdar was passionate about addressing the complex nature of hunger and poverty in Bangladesh.

For decades, Bangladesh had been subject to famine, cyclones, floods and a level of corruption that saw Transparency International rate them at the top of the list of most corrupt countries for several years running. But why?

In the early 90's, Majumdar was intrigued by a Wall Street Journal article by economist and professor Anne Osborn Krueger, which observed that South Korea and Bangladesh were in a similar state of development in 1971. Both countries had a hundred dollar per capita income, and the export share of GDP was comparable. South Korea had no resources other than some low-quality coal, and yet by 1991, it outmatched Bangladesh in quality of life, longevity, educational, governance and financial indices.

Majumdar was curious to understand how South Korea had developed so well, while his own country was seen so piteously in the international community.

For an economist, his conclusion was human-centred: 'After the 1971 Liberation War (where Bangladesh, then East Pakistan, fought off the army of West Pakistan to claim sovereignty after centuries of British and then Pakistani rule), we lacked the right kind of leadership. We forgot what we had learned – namely, that people matter, and people, if they take responsibility and action, can make anything happen.'

Majumdar was committed to making a difference in his country, so he returned home in 1991 with his wife Tazima and their five children.

For two years, Majumdar travelled Bangladesh, studying the country he had left more than twenty years before. His transformative realisation was that Bangladesh's most significant resource to end hunger were the hungry themselves. They were not the problem – they were the solution.

Majumdar identified that the biggest obstacle to progress, especially poverty alleviation, was how people thought about themselves and what they could do. In other words, their mindsets. He believed changing mindsets would catalyse progress for a better future and that achieving this would have to be centred around the leadership of the hungry themselves. In 1994, under Majumdar's supervision, wide-scale leadership training to shift mindsets swept the country of more than 160 million people.

To begin this process, he and his team developed a series of programs, the first of which was a half-day training with the villagers called the Vision, Commitment and Action workshop. The purpose was to identify the mindsets holding people back and create a new vision for their lives that was free from hunger.

I remember sitting in my first of these in 1998. People had come long distances – walking, on buses, and noisy scooters. Some of the women who attended had rarely left the confines of their small bamboo homes, yet here they were at a meeting on developing the leadership and mindsets to end hunger! Religious leaders shared how the concept of people having agency to care for their families was rooted in the religious texts they held sacred. Women were seated at the front and encouraged to share their views. Men grappled with old mindsets that said 'protecting' their daughters meant not educating them and marrying them off young.

Coming together, these resource-poor people wrestled with beliefs, stories and even their identity. They questioned assumptions about their inabilities that they had long held to be true, without ever considering the origin of those beliefs. Common limiting mindsets included, 'It's always been this way,' 'It's up to the government – we can't do this ourselves,' and 'Nothing will change, and there is nothing we can do about that.'

> They questioned assumptions about their inabilities that they had long held to be true, without ever considering the origin of those beliefs.

Majumdar and his team tapped into the nation's pride, recalling their incredible victory in the Liberation War that gave them their independence. Men and women had defied the odds against a superior force and were celebrated and revered as freedom fighters. Could the people of Bangladesh now become the next generation of 'freedom fighters' – this time liberating their country from hunger and poverty?

The discussion generated much excitement and tangible outcomes. This community identified building toilets as a priority – an absolute necessity in a country with limited access to safe sanitation – and created a work plan to build some latrines in the village.

This was a big deal. For decades they had been bypassed by progress, let down by waves of unfulfilled government promises, and burdened with entrenched and seemingly permanent poverty. These women and men had given up on change ever happening – until now.

In the following weeks, people gathered for their first mobilising activity. Amidst the laughter and pride, you could see their determination to get this done. Working together, they built several communal latrines, then went door-to-door to talk to their neighbours about the benefits of using the toilet instead of the field.

People were excited about what they had created. Yes, a government should provide sanitation for its people, but in its absence, the community had done it themselves. This achievement was the first win in a series of many that resulted in that village being free from hunger.

Over nearly thirty years, millions of people have participated in this mindset training – developed by Majumdar and his team and run by trained Bangladeshi volunteers. Students, politicans, householders, workers, and farmers from across the country have taken action to end hunger. Not to wait but to do it themselves. Women's collectives have formed. Literate folk taught others to read and write. Money was pooled to start small businesses. Widespread action stopped child marriages, stopped trafficking to neighbouring India, and stopped corruption from spreading through the nation. GDP went up. Access to sanitation improved. Girls stayed longer in school. So many outcomes resulted from this decision to start with mindsets.

Fast forward to 2009 when I was standing in a village outside Dhaka with my friend Michael Rennie, who was the Global Head of Organisational Transformation at international consulting firm

McKinsey & Co. He looked around at the activity and the mindsets generating it, shaking his head. 'I do a lot of work with large corporates, and we find that there are a couple of concepts people have to take in before you get change in a big organisation. One of them is moving from an external locus of control, where 'it's happening to me', to an internal one where you think 'I can make the change'. That's what they're doing here (in Bangladesh), and they're doing it in a similar way to how we do it with the biggest companies around the world, and for a fraction of the cost. It's amazing.'

Circumstances didn't need to turn favourable for the villagers to begin. What changed was their mindsets. They began to *lead in*.

> ## Circumstances didn't need to turn favourable for the villagers to begin. What changed was their mindsets.

Mindset for high performance

It's not just villages that have seen leadership blossom and outstanding outcomes through focusing on mindsets. Organisations and elite athletes utilise the same power.

When Satya Nadella became Microsoft's third-ever CEO in 2014, it's fair to say the business was not at its zenith. Over previous years, Microsoft had stalled as a pioneer and innovator. Nadella had inherited an organisation with a performance culture that pitted its people against each other. In his book *Hit Refresh*,[11] Nadella writes that 'staffers were rewarded not just for doing well but for making sure their colleagues failed'. Internally there was a culture of superiority, silos, and a fear of failure. This was reflected in its share price, which had stagnated for a decade.

Product launches were irregular, and few were successful. Bing couldn't match Google search, and Zune couldn't shake the Apple iPod. There was little appetite to try new things and launch new products. Microsoft was still a behemoth, but its current path risked diminishing what it had once been.

So what to do? In *Hit Refresh*, Satya Nadella describes how he focused deliberately on transforming the mindset within Microsoft. Specifically, the key limiting mindset was identified as being 'know-it-alls' – which means you have to be the smartest person in the room. You have something to prove. Being a genius is your identity! You went to the best schools and now work for an elite tech company – you cannot fail! This mindset was a huge block to the renewal desperately needed at Microsoft, so changing it became Nadella's priority.

As a counterpoint to being a know-it-all, Microsoft adopted the mindset of *learners*, or *learn–it–alls*. That means you are curious to learn new things. You understand that failing is important – it gives you the data necessary for growth and refinement. A learner is happy to work with others. They want the best outcome and are mature enough to acknowledge they don't know everything and that working with others increases success. Shifting the organisation from know-it-all's to *learn–it–alls* was crucial to Microsoft's turnaround.

The results speak for themselves. 'By developing a leadership mindset, managers and team members become more positive, innovative, open and engaged despite the tsunami of constant change. Focusing on mindsets is the reason Nadella gives for the share price doubling in just four years.'[12]

Mindsets for sporting high performance

At the time of writing, Ashleigh Barty is the world number one women's tennis player. Like many high performers, she has a mindset coach on her team. Hers is a man called Ben Crowe. 'Crowey' has shared his insights on the role mindset makes for elite performance.[13]

One of his core questions is, 'Do the conditions determine your mindset?' He believes they do not. If you let your environment or life situation determine your mindset, then those conditions can take you off course and leave you focused on the wrong things.

Crowe's work with Barty and other athletes is about learning to let go of what you can't control, and focusing on what you can control. This is very hard for any leader committed and passionate about an outcome. Yet, in sport, as in life, many outcomes can't be controlled. On the court, winds change. Stuff happens. Crowe says the only two things you can control are your intentions (strategy and tactics in Barty's case) and your mindset.

Barty's rise to world number one nearly didn't happen. Crowe shared the story of Barty at the French Open in 2019, where she had lost a set that should have been unlosable. Barty was three-love down in the next set and tension was high. She sat down to regroup, then started laughing! Her mindset shift was obvious to her coach – he could see that Ash recognised she was letting her environment determine her mindset. Instead, in a masterful example of *leading in,* she reframed it quickly: 'Uh-huh. I decide my mindset. I decide my attitude. I decide my self-worth. I decide.'

'I decide my mindset. I decide my attitude. I decide my self-worth. I decide.'

Now let's pause here for a moment. The pressure was excruciating. The world was watching. The focus on winning must have been immense. The environment was a huge arena for distraction with missed serves, umpire calls, and a global audience of millions. Yet Barty's focus shift was on her mindset – the only thing she could control. With this attitude change, she regrouped. She tended to her inner choices. Barty won the match and went on to win the French Open. Two weeks later, she won the Birmingham Classic in England and became the world number one.

Most of us don't perform anywhere near Barty's elite level, yet we also face challenges and obstacles that distract us. We get frustrated, focusing our efforts on the things in our environment that we can't change, and overlooking our mindset to our detriment. We forget that even when things are tough – maybe we're not meeting goals at work, or a family member is ill, or we are worried about the uncertainty in the world – our conditions don't determine our mindset.

We do. You do.

Especially when the stakes are high, the most powerful approach to success is to *lead in*.

Key points

- Your mindset is not you. You have a history of seeing yourself in a certain way, and while this feels true, these beliefs are not who you are.

- Focusing on external conditions does not give you access to power. Conditions will condition! The power lies in noticing what you are saying and believing about your relationship to those conditions.

- Addressing mindsets is crucial for working with complexity. Mindsets are the lever to shift challenges in your organisation, your community, and even in global challenges. Without this, nothing sustainable will happen.

- You can develop new mindsets that empower you. You can leave old beliefs behind. You get to write the story of what you are about.

Questions to consider

- Which mindset most holds you back?
- Without this mindset, what could you do?

Three

Four Mindsets

Carol Dweck's research identified two primary mindsets – fixed and growth. A fixed mindset has you thinking you only have the collection of skills you were gifted with at birth and can't develop any others. A growth mindset understands that skills and traits are not inherent and that you can improve and acquire mastery through practice.

The most exciting factor of Dweck's research (validated in hundreds of other experiments) is that mindsets can change. If you have a fixed mindset in an area, perhaps a belief that your work must be perfect before showing it to others, you are not fated to remain that way forever. This belief and the consequences that flow from it can change.

That doesn't mean you can do absolutely anything as long as you have the right mindset (you won't become a world-class pianist or a marathon runner next week). However, it does mean that continual improvement is possible, even in those areas where you thought you weren't naturally gifted. So, while I may never get to concert level excellence, I can improve my piano playing and learn more complicated pieces with practice and application. We can always learn, be curious and evolve.

All this goes against what many of us were told. As kids and young adults, we're urged to figure out what we're good at and double down on it. Spending time on anything else is seen as a waste. We are warned of failure if we don't stick with what we already do well.

We all have stories of being told something about our abilities – and believing it. It might have been 'you're no good with numbers' or 'art is for others (not you)' or 'you're sporty not smart'. We believed it because young minds are impressionable. We took these comments or opinions as truths about who we were, and they became part of our personality.

The flip side of caring

One of my clients is an intelligent and ambitious woman called Fumiko. She has accomplished a great deal in her career, including being on the team that managed the rollout of a significant piece of software that we all use today.

Fumiko worked with me because her manager believed she had the potential to be a good leader but was held back by her hesitancy to have tough conversations with her team. Fumiko agreed with this assessment. She dreaded having a performance discussion with one of her team members, who consistently missed deadlines. Fumiko couldn't bring herself to have the discussion. She didn't want him to see her as mean or unlikeable, and this reluctance held them both back.

In exploring what mindset might be in play, Fumiko reflected that she'd always been described as caring and helpful. This was high praise in her Japanese family, and Fumiko liked being this person for her parents and friends. She realised that this view of herself was still dominant, and while it was true, it wasn't the whole story of who she was. Her kind, caring, and helpful identity meant she avoided difficult conversations as she didn't want to rock the boat or make others feel uncomfortable.

Narrowing her view of herself to only being caring and helpful didn't give her the authority to rise as a leader. Leaders care, but they must also have courageous conversations. Recognising that this mindset did not completely define her allowed Fumiko to expand her view of herself and what she was capable of. She didn't have to stay boxed in this old identity. This realisation gave her the confidence to step up her leadership and support her team to lead more effectively. Fumiko had the much-needed conversation with her direct report, and while it felt clumsy and awkward, she recognised this was a skill she could develop. In pursuing her expanded sense of self, Fumiko accepted, rather than avoided, the discomfort these new behaviours initially triggered.

Fixed Mindset	Growth Mindset
Believes you can't change	Believes you can change
Skills are inherent	You can learn new things
Prioritises success (to avoid failure)	Prioritises growth (failing gives new information)
Hides flaws	Owns vulnerability and humanity
Avoids effort	Effort is the path to mastery
Seeks to prove	Wants to improve
Threatened by another's success	Inspired when others succeed
I know	I'm curious

Figure 1: Fixed and growth mindsets

Fixed mindset

The fixed and growth mindsets Dweck researched are found in everyone, though one might be more prevalent than the other, depending on the context.

A fixed mindset believes you have a particular set of skills and experiences to navigate life with. You have a finite amount of talent in your toolbox and think you're born with some skills and abilities and without others. When you try maths, and it goes well, you decide, 'yeah, I'm pretty good at this'. So that's what you focus on and can even build an identity around. If it keeps going well, you might make a career of it, shutting out other alternatives because *this* is what you are good at. You don't move too far from what you know.

The myth of natural talent

With a fixed mindset, you don't practise to master a skill because, well, if you're not already a 'natural', why would you?

For years I believed in the myth of natural talent and avoided the effort it took to develop mastery. I felt that if I needed to practise, it should remain secret as I didn't want people to think I struggled. I was ashamed if I was not immediately good at something in my job, especially if I thought CEOs 'should' be able to easily do it, such as public speaking or reading a profit and loss statement. I winged it a lot, causing myself unnecessary stress and anxiety. I didn't understand that this was down to my fixed mindset.

Avoiding activities where you might fail is the hallmark of a fixed mindset. Failure is devastating. Not only did the project or initiative fail, but *I failed too*! It becomes personal – *I am a failure*! If this mindset sounds familiar, you likely find yourself reducing your exposure to failure and becoming risk-averse. This might look like spending too much time planning and strategising because your endeavour must be entirely bulletproof before testing your proposition. And if you do put yourself out there and fail, your fixed mindset reinforces the same old thinking, so when another opportunity comes up, you decline. Whether an opportunity at work or in your personal life, you think, 'I'll never do that again. I tried it once, and it was an embarrassing failure.'

> Not only did the project or initiative fail, but *I failed too*! It becomes personal – *I am a failure*!

Being clever doesn't make you smart

Needing to be the cleverest person in the room, or a know-it-all, as the team at Microsoft called it, is part of a fixed mindset. But being clever doesn't always make you smart.

When you think you know everything about a particular subject, you close off being open to learning anything further. You know! You won't be told, and nothing will surprise you. This is a trap in relationships, especially when we've known someone for a while. Learning something new or deepening your knowledge becomes less available. When this mindset prevails, you can exhibit a lack of humility – you are always right, and you always know. It hardens over time into an inability to admit that you don't know something. When your identity is caught up in what you know, it's threatening to acknowledge areas where you are not the expert.

This mindset is common in leaders who have made careers out of what they know and what they've done. Yet, it is a mistake to rest here. As challenges grow in complexity, this mindset is a massive hindrance to activating ideas, collaborations and pursuit of the possible. As Albert Einstein is reputed to have remarked: 'We can't solve problems by using the same kind of thinking we used when we created them.' He knew that always proving how smart you are isn't very clever.

When we lead out, we focus on cementing our legitimacy and regard any questioning of our ideas or experience as a personal affront. A *lead in* leader knows that being right isn't what's important. They recognise that knowledge can always be gained, grown and integrated. They understand that giving up positionality doesn't diminish them. Indeed, it opens a leader up to new possibilities, inputs and pathways for creative action.

A *lead in* leader knows that being right isn't what's important.

Prioritising your success to avoid failing is another fixed mindset. There are different ways this can look. For some, it's sticking with what you know and are good at, even if it no longer brings you joy. You hesitate to branch out and try a new approach if there's a chance it won't work. Unfortunately, what got you this far won't get you to where you want to be. If you prioritise what works now over what you need to learn and grow to accomplish something bigger or more fulfilling, you may become irrelevant.

Others make decisions based on what is good for them rather than the business or mission. This has significant implications for people in leadership roles who have reached a level of success and want to hold on to it. I once worked with a team leader in a large organisation who had this mindset. Whenever the team suggested potential new markets that he wasn't familiar with, he would beat them down. He knew what he was good at and where he shone, and kept the business parameters in that narrow lane. His need for success overrode what was best for the group.

This mindset is also evident in any organisation that sticks with what it's known for and doesn't take risks or leaps to innovate and grow. In an ever-changing world, doing so signals decline, increasing irrelevancy and even collapse.

Picking your lane

With fixed mindsets, people pick their lane and stick to it. We capitalise on our specialty or what we think our talents are to the exclusion of all else. Over time this lane gets narrower and narrower even as life widens. We might have coasted on natural strength at school, but others will have similar or greater aptitudes or skills when we emerge into a broader life. Without recognising this, life and its possibilities shrink. And that is such a shame. At the very time when we need you to step into your leadership abilities, a fixed mindset limits the sphere you play in.

We overlay vulnerability with a mask that rarely comes off.

With a fixed mindset, we hide our flaws. We overlay vulnerability with a mask that rarely comes off. We feel we can't share when we're struggling or need help. We feel we 'should' be able to succeed, and to let others know we're only human will be detrimental in some way. That makes sense if we believe those are flaws (and not just part of being human), or imperfections that can never be changed or improved. The logic goes – 'if I am not good at something, I need to hide this from people'. It can even seem like a business risk to share our humanity with others.

Tim told me that he felt out of place in a business group of CEOs. He runs a successful boutique recruitment firm and joined the group to meet other business owners like him. He believed everyone there was so talented and accomplished that he couldn't let down his façade of success, energy and achievement – even for a moment. It was exhausting to be there, but Tim felt he had to protect his image or risk his business.

He had bought into a mindset that his struggles are unusual and even shameful, signifying some deep flaw. While this felt personal to Tim, I reckon many others were doing the same – spending all that energy to look serene gliding across the water while paddling madly and ungracefully below the surface. With a mindset of hiding his humanness, Tim won't get the friendship and support he is looking for. When we project that we always have it together, there is no opening for true partnership.

Like all mindsets, fixed mindsets are contextual. That means you might be tough and inscrutable at work, always hiding what's going on, but with your friends, you are a big soft bunny rabbit, open and trusting. You might be curious in your studies, but a know-it-all when it comes to your teenage children. You might believe that your colleague will grow and learn from a failure, but convinced your partner will never change. It's confusing, isn't it? That's because we humans are messy, complicated creatures!

So it's good to remember that a *lead in* leader doesn't fixate on their fixed mindsets. They know this is not who they are. They are aware they can move into more empowering mindsets at any time.

Growth mindset

The counter point to the fixed mindset is a growth mindset, which understands that talent and skills can be learned and grown. Dweck's research showed that you can develop in any area you choose with attention and practice. It does not guarantee that you'll become an Olympic level athlete, but it does mean that you can improve from the base where you started.

A growth mindset is when you believe you have the capacity to enhance your abilities, learn new skills, build on existing skills, or even try something completely new.

As Dweck explains, 'The passion for stretching yourself and sticking to it, even (or especially) when it's not going well, is the hallmark of the growth mindset. It allows people to thrive during some of the most challenging times in their lives.'[14]

A growth mindset loosens failure's grip. While few of us like to fail, doing so is simply data to develop your ideas and strategies further. You are more interested in what you learn and how you grow by trying new things than the pressure of thinking you have only one shot – and it better work.

Similarly, a growth mindset encourages curiosity. You don't have to prove you are right or defend your position. You think through your ideas and can rethink them when new information comes to hand. You are not searching for data that only supports your current view. You know you don't have to know everything, and indeed you never will. You can easily say, 'I'm not sure, I'll find out' when asked a question you can't answer. You want to learn and evolve.

> You think through your ideas
> and can rethink them when new
> information comes to hand.

Being human

Owning your vulnerability and humanity is a powerful aspect of this mindset. We are all human, yet so much energy goes into pretending we have it all together. Instead, accepting that we are continually growing and will mess up from time to time offers respite from the stress and energy it takes to maintain the facade. And when you do mess up, you have compassion for yourself.

Lead in leaders know this. Rather than keeping up the appearance of omnipotence and all-knowing, they acknowledge their fears and concerns. They make mistakes and don't have all the answers. They own what it means to be human.

I worked with the leadership team at a mission-driven and highly stressful organisation. There, a team member shared a profound interaction she'd had with her boss, who was also learning how to *lead in*. The day after a meeting that didn't go well, her boss called and apologised. 'Ana, I didn't like how I was in our meeting yesterday. I was feeling under the pump, and it was unfair to you. I'm sorry, and I will do better in our next one-on-one.' Far from showing weakness, he modelled vulnerable leadership, and in doing so, gave Ana permission to show up more courageously and wholeheartedly.

A fixed mindset feels threatened by another's success, while a growth mindset is inspired when others do well. Gore Vidal's maxim 'Whenever a friend succeeds, a little something in me dies' speaks to that small, mean part of being human that sometimes rears its head. Yet being genuinely inspired and excited at the success of others is a growth mindset worth encouraging. It lays the foundation for continued accomplishment in areas that matter to us.

Mindsets do not depend on circumstances

You may imagine we can only have a growth mindset when things are going well, but that isn't the case. For example, you might find it confronting to speak up in meetings at work. With a fixed mindset, you stay quiet and say to yourself, 'I'm not a good speaker', 'I don't want to look foolish', or 'They won't want to hear my opinion'. If pushed, you might try, but if it doesn't go well, you think, 'There, I knew I shouldn't have tried that. I'm not good enough to get my point across.' So you stay quiet because you believe you don't have that ability.

In this next example, the situation is the same. You feel shy to talk in meetings, but your growth mindset means you persevere because you know it is important. You know that speaking in meetings, building influence, and getting your voice heard is something you need to do better. Even though you may lack specific skills and experiences to do this well, you know you can develop them with practice and perseverance. Even if the first few attempts are unsuccessful, you say, 'Oh, that didn't go well. Next time I'll speak more clearly, or not wait till the end'. You know that every attempt brings more data points to learn from, and you improve.

Limited and expansive mindsets

In my work first with The Hunger Project, and then developing leaders in organisations, I saw another way to think about mindsets. It adds perspective to Dweck's growth and fixed concepts by focusing on mindsets for creating broader scale change. I call them limited and expansive mindsets.

Limited mindsets underpin much of the leadership thinking holding back our organisations and our responses to challenging social, political and ecological conditions. Expansive mindsets offer ways to overcome these and develop the people capacity and personal confidence to step up. We use expansive mindsets when we *lead in*.

Limited Mindset	Expansive Mindset
I can't lead / they can't lead	Everyone can make an impact
Scarcity thinking	Inner resources are our greatest asset
Limitations are the excuse	Limitations provide focus and new ideas
Disempowered and resigned	Empowered and accountable
Past dictates future	Past informs. Future is to be created.
This is how things are done around here	We can create new ways
Don't feel like it	Feeling follows action
Closed	Open
Impossible	Possible

Figure 2: Limited and expansive mindsets

Limited mindsets

Limited mindsets are the beliefs and stories that keep us small and contained. They restrict our horizons, reducing what we think can be accomplished. They keep us impotent in expressing our power to bring about meaningful change. With this mindset, we can see every reason why something won't work and isn't possible. Thoughts of expansion or a new possibility leave us overwhelmed or frustrated. When up against obstacles, we feel defeated and ask, 'why bother?'

One of the most damaging limited mindsets is that only some people can lead. This views leadership as a skill you either have or don't. And if you don't have it, it can't be developed. Many things limit ideas about leadership and who wields it, and unexamined cultural conditioning is a big one. When we think 'leader', who are we seeing?

One of the most damaging limited mindsets is that only some people can lead.

For too long, leadership has been regarded as a collection of traits, chosen by what diversity expert Michelle King calls 'the prototype'.[15] This prototype fits a narrow definition: it's usually cis male, heterosexual, married, and (in a Western context) white. It exudes characteristics of extroversion, dominance, charisma, boldness. Most people unconsciously agree that these traits make someone a natural leader. If you don't have them, then you're not. It's sobering to see how ingrained this narrow view of leadership is.

Resetting perceptions

Examining assumptions about leadership brought a surprising insight for one participant at a team offsite I ran. Britt is an executive who holds a lot of responsibility. She built a profitable arm for a leading retail organisation and led her team with grit and heart. Yet Britt struggled with a lack of confidence, and her fears diluted attention she could have directed toward her operations.

Britt's beliefs about who could lead were getting in her way. It turned out that Britt didn't lack confidence. Instead, she was measuring herself against a rigid, normalised view of leadership that she didn't fit. Like many women, she wasn't confident within that old paradigm. Instead of critiquing that outdated model and owning her leadership style, Britt was stuck in a disempowered view of herself.

Limiting our ideas about leadership reinforces prevailing structures. We lock out the multiplicity of perspectives, people and experiences needed to strengthen our societies and organisations. Too many amazing people reduce their impact because they tap themselves out before starting. It is deficit thinking: we get sidetracked trying to fit some unattainable ideal instead of leading in our unique and unleashed way.

> Limiting our ideas about leadership reinforces prevailing structures.

That's what was happening for Britt. She felt she was falling short when comparing herself to her dynamic CEO and her internalised ideas of who leaders are. It makes perfect sense because Britt had not yet figured out her voice as a leader. Her limited mindset meant she only saw what she wasn't – not what she was or could be. Empowered with this realisation, Britt focused on owning her unique way of leading and all she had accomplished. Britt didn't need fixing, and she wasn't lacking confidence. Instead, she stepped into a new paradigm of leading that became a far more effective and energising path to explore.

The past limits possibilities

A limited mindset projects the past into the present and future, so what you want to do and who you think you can be gets tied up (or bogged down) in history. When thinking about the future or a new idea, a limited mindset immediately closes off or narrows possibilities that are outside your experience. It shows up in beliefs like 'We tried it before and it didn't work', 'It's never been done before', and 'This is how things are done around here'. This mindset is like driving a car and navigating through the rear-view mirror. You can only see where you have gone. The future is not available to you.

Of course, that does not suggest you ignore what has gone before. That would be nuts. Being informed by the past makes sense. But the limited mindset is only interested in that, checking its memory drive to see what you have already done. This stifles growth and progress because it restricts our course of action to what has already worked or what we already know.

We all fall prey to past-based thinking from time to time. You want to find a partner, but 'I went on a couple of dates, and they were terrible, so I'll never find anyone.' Or you see a cool initiative in another company but don't take it further because 'Our organisation always turns down these kinds of things,' thus giving up before you even start. Or you want to take up painting as a creative outlet, but you feel so embarrassed at how bad you remember being in high school art classes that you don't try.

Scarcity thinking is another key indicator of a limited mindset. This mindset is so fundamental and widespread that I have devoted Chapter Seven to it. It is the belief that there is not enough of something crucial (time, money, people) to succeed. It often sounds like, 'If only we had X, then we'd achieve our goal.'

This limited mindset showed up for a team at a major bank. They were hurtling toward their end of financial year deadlines, and morale was low. People could not see how they could meet their targets and were in the grip of scarcity. Their pervasive, collective mindset said there was not enough time, days, clients or bandwidth to achieve their goals.

Although intelligent and committed, the team could not see any possibility because the circumstances seemed too difficult. Whatever action they took was coloured by this mindset, which is why the team leader invited me to work with them. The transformation required a shift in mindset. I'll share more about how that happened in the next section, but for now, notice where you too get caught in a similar scarcity mindset, finding reasons why things that are important to you can't happen because of something you lack.

Limited mindsets show up in the blame game. When you find yourself blaming others, complaining, or wishing life was another way, you can be sure you have a limited mindset. Blaming others is the move of a weak leader. It might feel like it's assigning responsibility to another person or a particular event when things don't work out as you wanted. Yet even if your reasoning is valid, blaming does not give you access to the power needed to resolve your problem. Instead, blaming others lets you off the hook. If it's not your fault, then there's nothing you can do.

Not feeling it

One of the myths around leadership is that you need to feel confident, inspired or energised to make a move. You wait for your feelings to match the action you need to take, and if you act without the corresponding feeling, you're not being 'authentic'. This mindset says that if you feel nervous about leading, you shouldn't put your hand up for a new role. If you feel shy, then that's your cue to stay quiet.

Letting your feelings dictate how you show up is not a good leadership strategy.

Letting your feelings dictate how you show up is not a good leadership strategy – especially when you're dealing with something fraught, complex and challenging. In those times, if you're waiting for feelings of confidence before taking action, you might be waiting a long time. This limited mindset waits for inspiration to call, and if it doesn't, you don't do anything.

Opportunities for growth and development are mightily hindered if you only take them when you're feeling it. That doesn't mean ignoring your feelings. As you'll see when we get to the Mindset Process in Chapter Six, paying attention to them is critical. However, this limited mindset is only interested in keeping you small and not subjecting you to the discomfort that growth necessitates. The mindset wins when you elevate feelings over growth and discovery.

Being closed

A limited mindset is closed to new ideas or ways of thinking. This shows when organisations get caught in a bubble of groupthink and don't check with their customers and markets.

In his book *Think Again*,[16] Adam Grant shares the gripping story of how Mike Lazaridis, creator of the once-ubiquitous Blackberry, fell victim to being closed off to the critical ways smartphone technology was changing. Lazaridis was, by all accounts, a genius, yet he was not open to any version of the Blackberry that did not have a keyboard. His fans and acolytes loved this feature, but, as history shows, the glass screen became the dominant tech.

Blackberry's global market share dropped from twenty per cent in 2009 to less than five per cent in 2012. In the last quarter of 2016, Blackberry's smartphone market share went to zero per cent, with fewer than 300,000 units sold globally.[17]

> # Being smart is no guarantee that you will be open.

Being closed to new ideas, thinking, and ways of leading is a classic limited mindset that can ruin the best of us. Being smart is no guarantee that you will be open. When you know so much and are right so often, it's easier to close yourself off from ideas outside your wheelhouse and expertise. As Lazaridis discovered, in a world of incredible change, a closed mindset is a liability, not an asset.

The greatest threat

Most egregiously, limited mindsets blunt concerted, inspired action on things that really matter. When addressing issues like racism, patriarchy or ecological devastation, the limited mindset is a huge obstacle to creating a wave of creative, courageous change. As environmentalist Robert Swan said, 'The greatest threat to our planet is the belief that someone else will save it.'[18] If you believe things really can't change and anything new is impossible, any action you take will be constrained and tainted with hopelessness.

'The greatest threat to our planet is the belief that someone else will save it.'

The devastating consequence of this mindset is evident around approaches to global issues like hunger and climate change. A limited mindset sees hunger as 'It's always been here, and it will never change.' With climate change, it whispers in your ear, 'There is nothing I or we can do. It's too late.' Yet if you believe that most people (including you) can't make a difference and that you are too small and too inconsequential to act, the current power structures will remain, without your influence ever brought to bear. If you see little evidence that humans are capable and courageous, then concerted and effective action on behalf of the systemic, complex issues that affect us all will not happen.

Many good people are caught in this aspect of the limited mindset. If things look unrelenting and hopeless, why should the future be any different? When you're constantly disappointed by government policies or dismayed by wilful misrepresentations, it would seem foolish to think that anything can change. With this mindset, action is mired in resignation and despair.

You see the limited mindset in organisations when people say, 'There's nothing I can do. This is just how things are done here.' You see it in villages, where people would say to me, 'We've always been hungry. This will never change.' And globally, when we tell ourselves, 'It's too late,' or 'The governments are too corrupt, nothing I do matters.' This mindset is killing our opportunity to solve the huge and urgent problems facing humanity and all species. And it does not speak the truth about who we really are.

Expansive mindsets

To *lead in* requires us to transform limited mindsets, and we do this by cultivating expansive ones.

The expansive mindset understands we all have the capacity to lead. And by lead, I mean making a difference and having an impact on something important to you. As we explored in Chapter Two, you don't need a title or even other people to be a leader. Anyone can impact and lead, even if they haven't done this before or are in a group of people traditionally denied leadership roles. The expansive mindset sees that leadership is possible – for you and for all.

With an expansive mindset, you view leadership like an electric current. When you flick the switch, the light comes on. When you flick it again, it goes off. The current – the potential for electricity – is always present. Leadership is the same, and everyone has access to this potential. Activated or dormant, the potential is there. The work is to empower yourself and your team to activate their leadership potential.

Not your personality

With an expanded mindset, leadership is something people can reach for. It's not a personality type. But how often do we get stuck on this idea that being a leader is a type?

Mel did. Fifteen years ago, she did a Myers Brigg personality assessment at a team offsite. The trainer explained that Mel's particular profile type meant she is great at supporting and inspiring others, but 'you don't see leaders with this combination. You won't ever lead anything yourself, but you'll always be a sought-after team member that the leader you're working with will rely on.'

Mel took those words to heart which made sense because they fit the typical narrative about leadership – that some can and most can't. As a result, she limited her career progression, sticking to roles that 'fit my type'. The expansive mindset rejects this perspective. The ability to lead is not like double-jointedness, which some people have and most don't. It's not your personality type. It took years for Mel to overcome this label and revel in her 'liberated leaderly Mel-ness', as she put it. As she discovered when she later set up her own organisation, employing five people and kicking her goals – leading is available to all.

Expansive mindsets empower.

Expansive mindsets empower. They enlarge our sense of what is possible and achievable, giving us room to play, create, innovate and achieve. They are not based on the past. You are not limited to what you know – you can embrace the unknowns. Instead of finding reasons why something can't be done, this mindset thinks 'What if?' or 'Why not?'

No sacred cows

Openness to new ideas, including being challenged about beliefs you hold dear, is a crucial aspect of the expansive mindset. Norms held as sacrosanct have been up-ended in just a few years. Expectations that everyone will work from an office or that it is impossible to get good work from people not under constant observation are being challenged. As we see, leaders who are open to new research, data, and hearing from their employees will keep great people in their organisations.

Human progress depends on reconsidering what you take for granted. Changes regarding racist and sexist views are great examples of this – people and societies are re-evaluating outdated beliefs and behaviours and choosing new ones. Failing to question yourself and your ideas will keep you fossilised.

Feeling follows action

The expansive mindset doesn't need to be in the mood to lead. The limited mindset waits for feelings to match the new space, yet the research is clear: feelings follow actions just as much as actions follow feelings. As Katty Kay and Claire Shipman write in their book *The Confidence Code*[19] 'Confidence accumulates through hard work, through success, and even through failure.' Put another way, taking action reinforces your belief in your ability to succeed.

Don't wait to be ready before
you move forward.

With this expansive mindset, a *lead in* leader understands that confidence is no indicator of readiness or ability. They say yes to uncomfortable growth opportunities, even if they feel hesitant or unsure. Don't wait to be ready before you move forward. This is far from being inauthentic. With an expansive mindset, you understand that your highest level of authenticity is being true to your potential as a human being. You take action based on that.

It's normal to have a lag in congruency between who you can be and how you feel about it. Expect that and reframe it as growth.

Hidden resources

The expansive mindset views resources and abilities in a fluid and generous way. It is the antidote to being frustrated and thwarted by your perceived limitations. Earlier we read about how an expansive mindset re-energised a bank team struggling with its targets and approach.

Rather than obsessing over the lack of results and difficult economic conditions, the team members regrouped around what they could control. They approached their clients differently. They used the time between calls to centre themselves and choose their mindset instead of reacting. They reorganised resources among the team, moving away from a siloed approach. New people managers who were recently analysts, were coached to get the best from their team, instead of criticising and micro-managing.

The team ended up meeting their targets and deadlines and did so in a way that left them pumped for the following year – not exhausted and wrung out. All through utilising the power of mindsets.

With an expansive mindset, circumstances and challenges are not overlooked or concealed. This isn't simply positive thinking. When deadlines are coming at you, you need to deal with the reality as it is. You don't spend time wishing things were different or looking for excuses or justifications. Instead, you clearly assess the conditions, mobilise the resources you do have and deploy them in new ways.

Imagination and possibility

This is particularly true when addressing complex problems. Many global issues feel insurmountable. Inequality and discrimination are embedded in many major institutions. We face the sixth mass extinction that threatens much of life as we know it on this planet. Struggles with mental health affect nearly everyone, either personally or in their family or friendship groups. There are many things happening in our world and our lives that are deeply worrying.

The power of the expansive mindset is the ability to confront this and not diminish your potency for action. Just because the odds seemed stacked against you and change seems slow or even non-existent, does not mean responsiveness is pointless. There are no guarantees, but the expansive mindset gives us heart. It has us think in terms of a 'bigger me' rather than the 'smaller me'. You seek new possibilities, tactics, actions and partnerships to achieve the goal. It allows you to multiply your effectiveness by working with others. It helps you to keep going.

The expansive mindset gives us heart.

Imagination is at the heart of an expansive mindset. Just because things haven't been done before, it doesn't mean they can't be done. There are new territories to explore, people to empower, unworkable structures to transform and new ways of leading. With an expansive mindset, you understand and resonate with so many possibilities.

Possibility thinking is part of this mindset. It upends resignation and the belief that nothing you do will change anything. The word possible has its origin in the Latin word *possibilis*, meaning 'that can be done'. I love this etymology! You can access possibility by asking, 'Who else can I work with on this? How can we see this differently? What might we imagine?'

An expansive mindset helps build the motivation and the momentum to turn things around. Unlike the limited mindset, which looks to the past for examples of how things never changed, the expansive mindset gives you the courage to envisage a better future. This vision is key to staying the course when things get hard.

To *lead in*, focus on what you want
and what is important to you – even
if you can't yet see the pathway.

To *lead in*, focus on what you want and what is important to you – even if you can't yet see the pathway. That incisive clarity, once found, will carve out multiple avenues to success. An expansive mindset gives you the agency and inner direction to get to work rather than being derailed by what's not working or not going to plan.

Key points

- Even if you have found it hard to move beyond a particular way of thinking, know that mindsets can change.

- We are a combination of all the mindsets – growth and fixed, expansive and limiting, with each triggered or activated by different contexts and conditions.

- When conditions are difficult, don't obsess over them, as this focuses you on the wrong target. Conditions will condition! Stuff happens! Instead, focus on your mindset. That is what you can control.

- Practise the corresponding growth or expansive mindset whenever you are stuck. Do this consciously to *lead in*.

Questions to consider

- Which fixed mindset most trips me up? Under what conditions or circumstances does it most show up?

- What corresponding growth mindset can I develop?

- Which limited mindset most trips me up? When does it most show up?

- What corresponding expansive mindset can I develop?

- How can I keep the growth and expansive mindsets I want, front of mind?

Four

The Leadership Quadrant

There have never been more challenges to leading effectively. The pandemic launched a situation that we can't control, and we face continual difficulties in our working lives. We might have a boss that constantly changes their mind and doesn't know what they are doing. We might be new to managing people and caught in a 'fake it til I make it' version of leading. We certainly face personal doubts and worries. All this is stressful and can push us to *lead out* to deal with it all. In doing so, we focus on external variables and ignore what's going on within us.

Difficult circumstances make it crucial to *lead in* and focus on what we can control, but this rarely happens without deliberate choice. As we will see, we can fall into lesser ways of getting things done when under pressure. These are our default leading mindsets, which we will explore in this chapter.

The fixed, growth, limited and expansive mindsets intersect in ways that can indicate your default leadership mindset. They come together in a quadrant, and here we'll look at three of them: Dictator, Victim and Delayer.

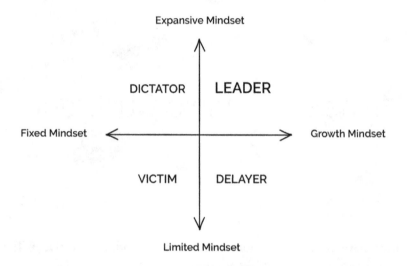

Figure 3: Mindset leadership styles

These leadership styles are not exhaustive, but they are common to most of us as an unconcious way of leading when things are tough. The Dictator, Victim and Delayer mindsets each have aspects that work, but they are sub-optimal ways of achieving your goals.

We'll look at each one in turn before examining the leadership style of a *lead in* leader – the Leader's mindset.

The Dictator mindset

Expansive and fixed mindsets meet in the upper left quadrant, which activates both qualities. The result is a leadership style that can become autocratic. I call it the Dictator because when leading from this place, you see a new vision of the future (expansive), but the way you go about it is rigid, exclusive and narrow (fixed).

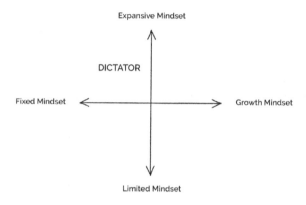

Figure 4: The Dictator mindset

Dictators don't trust others to do the job right. With a 'my way or the highway' attitude, they are unilateral decision-makers.

With this mindset, at some level, you believe that only you can do it.

If you resort to command-and-control under pressure, it's a sure sign that you're leading from this mindset. I find it's one of the most common default mindsets in high achievers and managers, and it's a huge source of frustration for people who work with and for them.

With this mindset, at some level, you believe that only you can do it. Others can't be trusted to accomplish what you are about. You have the vision, and it must be achieved your way. You are the only one who knows. Dictators see what is possible and are ambitious to achieve it, yet a fixed mindset means their thinking is narrow, and their leadership actions are reactive and limited.

It's not uncommon to find the Dictator mindset active in people new to management. It comes from the insecurity of not feeling good enough and worrying that others will find out. Less experienced managers can also be over-influenced by what passes as more traditional leadership styles and try to emulate them.

I work with many emerging leaders who are leading people for the first time. At one large firm, a number of analysts had been promoted to leading their first teams. Given the highly target-driven culture, plenty of Dictator behaviours were on display.

Anton was an experienced technician who was proud and excited about his promotion, but he found the role very stressful. People just weren't listening to him! He told his analysts what to do, and they would still mess it up somehow. He would then take over their tasks by micromanaging every detail or doing the work himself. Anton felt disrespected and frustrated, but his issue was always with the team members. Maybe he needed to recruit better people? They obviously weren't up to the job. Anton's experience is typical for someone leading with a Dictator mindset.

The Dictator leads from fear, and failure is one of their greatest fears. This was Anton – caught up in the excitement and challenge of his promotion, but he was also afraid. Anton wasn't completely sure he knew what he was doing, and he didn't want his boss to regret his decision to promote him. To mitigate this, Anton followed the leadership behaviours he had seen in others and became autocratic to get the job done.

The Dictator leads from fear, and failure is one of their greatest fears.

Dictators are alienating. They can fall into micromanaging, and one of their most significant resources (other people) drift away. They do not empower and develop others, and this makes sense because they believe skills are fixed. There's no point investing in someone if they don't already have the expertise! Dictators stifle the debate and conversation that is integral to solving complex issues. People are silenced and become disengaged around a Dictator.

Leading primarily with a Dictator mindset is like a splint worn too long that weakens the muscles. When people lead this way, their leadership bench thins. Learned helplessness seeps in, and good people leave. No one is empowered for long under this style of leadership.

For all their bravado, the Dictator mindset is often insecure, so leading this way bolsters ego and self-belief. In some cases, people truly believe they are worthy of the power they use to dominate and control. Having got to the top, they like it and want to stay. They are more interested in the position than in serving the mission or its people, and in some cases, they even regard the mission and people as serving their needs! With this mindset, you believe in your own hype. You don't think you have further to learn or grow. You're not humble.

There is no room for diversity of thought or nuance when leading with a Dictator mindset. Everything planned into the future is still an iteration of the past. Other people's leadership cannot blossom around a dictator.

In a nutshell, Dictators say, 'This is what you'll do.'

What happens when we lead this way

You are leading with a Dictator mindset when you:

- Work in a 'power over' way, which is top-down and tries to enforce or coerce the behaviours you want to see

- Lead through fear and control

- Feel insecure in your role, always on the lookout for being challenged (whether that's actually happening or not)

- Have a 'my way or the highway' attitude, or are a unilateral decision-maker

- Use your position to dominate and control others

- Think your ideas and plans are best and get upset if they are not followed

- Believe your authority is forever. You have an entitlement that your position will last for as long as you want it to. Anyone who challenges that, such as a star performer in your team, will be seen as a rival. In this way, Dictators are challenged by others with the potential to lead.

- Find it hard to accept the truth if it doesn't suit your narrative. You foster a culture where people don't tell you what's really going on, or they sugar coat it.

Benefits and cost

The Dictator isn't all bad news. Like all mindsets, it arises because it can serve a purpose. Many people who default to Dictator believe it is the only way to achieve results and get their team working productively. They may not like it, but they can't argue with the outcome.

I often hear good people share that they don't like being domineering, but they feel there is no other option when big deadlines loom. They say, 'When there is time pressure, and I need everyone to fall in line, I have to be a Dictator – otherwise we won't get anything done.'

The Dictator mindset can get the job done – but it's a short-term job.

There's no denying that the Dictator mindset can get the job done – but it's a short-term job. It handles the emergency. Like a firefighter telling us to step back from the fire, the authority imbued in this command makes us listen and do as we are told. It works, so we keep using it. It becomes the automatic mindset response, especially under pressure. And let's face it, most of us feel the pressure every day in our work and life, so it can be a difficult mindset to break.

Other benefits of leading with a Dictator mindset include decisiveness and impact. In some contexts, you are even admired! You also have control over vision and execution.

But the costs can be high.

The cost

Being a Dictator is not sustainable without enormous effort, resourcing and compliance. There is a real threat to the mission if the Dictator leaves, as there are not enough people empowered to take over. Conversely, there is a threat to the organisation if the person leading with the Dictator mindset stays and isn't guided to change their leadership style. The power they wield feels tentative, like building a house on sand. There's always a threat to be stamped out, and it's exhausting for everyone. Even if you have a great vision and mission, you will create resistance if you lead this way. There will be some quick wins, but you'll lose the war.

Why do we lead from Dictator?

We don't sit in the Dictator quadrant because we are monsters, but because unconscious drivers have taken us there. It's useful to notice what they are and see them within ourselves. You might fall into a Dictator mindset because something is important to you, and you're worried it won't happen if it's not done your way. You might see a gap in leadership and step in to fill it.

One of the myths that drive this mindset is a distorted view of effective leadership. Leading differently is regarded as nice-to-have, not a must-have. It's what we do when everything's going well. That is because we confuse leading from an expansive and growth mindset as somehow weaker – images of team retreats where we're singing Kumbaya spring to mind.

As we'll discover when we look at how to *lead in* with a Leader's mindset, nothing could be further from the truth.

Moving from a Dictator mindset

If you find yourself defaulting to the Dictator mindset, look to the quadrant axes to guide you. For the fixed axis, identify those primary mindsets that constrain. For instance, you might be prioritising success to avoid any failure. Or perhaps you believe your team don't have the skills, so you have to tell them what to do.

Now reframe these through the corresponding growth mindset. If you feel you have to hide your flaws and always show up as someone who has it together and is the font of all knowledge, practise softening into some of your vulnerabilities. Share your humanity and invite contribution and support from others. If you believe your team isn't talented enough, reflect on your own journey and how you've grown over time. You didn't start as the competent person you are now. Look to how your team can be empowered and encouraged with that insight. Discover what they are capable of when a Dictator does not lead them.

Now, look at the qualities on the expansive axis which Dictator already has access to. Consider which expansive mindsets you want to boost. It might be recognising the leadership capabilities in your people and supporting their competency by guiding them or increasing the scope of their role. Or it might be through sharing that you don't have the answers, but you believe that together the team has what it takes to figure out the best solution.

Focusing on the growth and expansive axes helps you *lead in*. It moves you from a Dictator to a Leader's mindset.

The Victim mindset

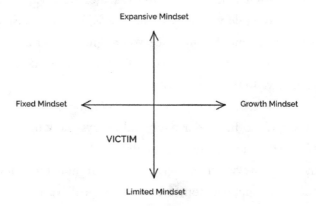

Figure 5: The Victim mindset

Perhaps under pressure, you don't default to the Dictator mindset, but instead, find yourself sliding into the bottom left quadrant where the Victim mindset lives. This is where the fixed and limited mindsets intersect. It is a life-leeching, thief of joy we can all (ahem) fall victim to. It is easily triggered by anything unwanted in your environment: a disappointing piece of news, tough feedback from your manager, not making your quarterly target or missing out on that promotion.

Let me be clear that a Victim mindset is not the same as being a victim. I use the word as a description of a mindset, not as a judgement or comment on people who are truly victims of events. The word *victim* can be misconstrued and misused. In this leadership context, Victim is a mindset, not a person. It is how we respond to an unfavourable situation. We can all feel like this from time to time.

Where Dictators say 'This is what you'll do', Victims say 'I don't know what to do. Tell me what to do.'

A powerless combination

The combination of fixed and limited mindsets can make it harder to shift as there is no growth or expansive axis to draw from. (Ironically, if you get stuck in a Victim mindset as your default, this can add to your sense of powerlessness. 'Of course, Victim doesn't have a 'good' axis in it!') When we have this mindset, everything that happens to or around us, even rainy weather, can feel like a personal afront.

With a Victim mindset, you believe you have no power to change anything. Your locus of control is external, not internal. You are leading out, always at the mercy of events, unable to access the agency and action to move forward. You wait and hope for things to change.

The Victim mindset is most affected by circumstances.

The Victim mindset is most affected by circumstances. When your attention is only on reacting to the conditions you are in, the game's already up. Focusing on how bad or unfair something is, or how terrible you feel about it, and why it shouldn't be so, keeps you in a Victim loop.

One team I worked with shared a Victim mindset regarding their organisation's head office, which was on a different continent, half a world away. While the local team worked well together, they felt powerless and blindsided by requests and timelines given to them by HQ. Team members complained that they couldn't possibly deliver without pulling all-nighters. They regarded the requests as unreasonable and making no sense. They felt disrespected, marginalised, and invisible. Language and cultural differences added further barriers. It seemed nothing they did made any difference.

The Victim mindset kept the team resentful and on the back foot. You can see in this example how the quadrant axes plays out: the fixed mindsets of 'That's just the way the people at HQ are – they'll never change', along with the limited mindsets of 'There's nothing we can do, it's just not possible.'

The team's frustration seemed perfectly reasonable from where they were sitting. (I even had some sympathy for them, as an Australia-based CEO who had worked with a head office in New York, this scenario resonated!) However, in thinking through their issue from a *lead in* perspective, they could see that 'It's being done to me' was not a powerful way to run a business.

It's easy to spot when the Victim mindset grinds you down. Like Snow White's dwarves, Victim has (at least) seven draining companions:

- Helpless: 'I can't do this. Please tell me what to do.'

- Overwhelm: 'I don't know where to start. It's all too much.'

- Hopeless: 'There's no point, it will never work.'

- Judgement: 'Who's fault is this? It's not my fault. It shouldn't be this way.'

- Resignation: 'It's all too hard. It will never change.'

- Blame: '*They* should do something about that.'

- Complaint: 'Why is this happening? It's not fair.'

When you hear or see any of these, you can be confident that a Victim mindset is in town.

What happens when you lead this way

When you're leading from a Victim mindset:

- You waste energy complaining and wishing things were different.

- You spend time catastrophising, building issues into insurmountable hurdles. You run around getting everyone worked up. There is lots of drama because if everything is outside your control, you make problems larger to get the help and attention you feel you need.

- You lack accountability. You pass the buck. If it's someone else's fault, how can anyone blame you for not coming through with the goods?

- You bring others down to your level. This can be through gossiping and bitching – usually about the people below who aren't delivering or the people above who are incompetent and uncaring. All according to you, of course.

José is an executive in a medium-sized education company that had recently hired a new CEO, Mike. José ran a regional wing of the business and knew it inside out. He enjoyed great relationships with his colleagues and customers. He was initially excited by the hire of the new CEO, but over time he became frustrated with decisions made. He felt the new guy just didn't get the business. José knew others felt the same, and discontent seemed to grow over time. Exciting announcements were made, then nothing was mentioned again. Some people were favoured over others. Results stagnated.

The Victim mindset doesn't always look like someone weeping in the corner.

José started feeling bitter and resentful about the directors who had hired the CEO, and Mike himself. He and others complained together and rolled their eyes in meetings when Mike spoke. While José was still passionate about his role and serving his customers well, his influence was not positive. José was leading from a Victim mindset. He had a fixed view of not accepting any flaws in his CEO or allowing room for mistakes and learning. He was limited in that he couldn't see that he could support and enhance Mike's leadership.

The Victim mindset doesn't always look like someone weeping in the corner. It can be a very powerful mindset, although the results are not positive. Although it was hard for José to admit, he recognised that, with this mindset, he was actively undermining the CEO, creating drama about the organisation's future, and bringing others along with him – all to the detriment of the company. His story is not unique. When you don't have a say in decisions that affect you, a default response is to find agency where you can. This might be through gossiping, spreading stories, forming silos of opinions, and complaining in a way that doesn't make any difference.

Mindset with benefits

Although it's not a nice place to be, there are benefits to leading from a Victim mindset. You have an excuse for failing – or at least not trying. If you really believe you are hopeless and inept, you will never put yourself out there, and this keeps you safe from criticism.

You can't be blamed for not delivering if you have promoted the narrative that it's all outside your control. It minimises your risk (something the fixed mindset seeks) and validates why you think change is impossible and not worth working toward (something the limited mindset seeks).

And as we saw in José's case, you can generate activity to feel you are doing something. It's just not the sort of activity that will make any difference, so feelings of powerlessness prevail.

One of the greatest benefits of a Victim mindset is that it stops others from calling you to account.

One of the greatest benefits of a Victim mindset is that it stops others from calling you to account. People hesitate to have a tough conversation with someone in a Victim mindset. When you are in overwhelm or facing difficult conditions, it's easy for others to agree with you. In creating a 'poor you' identity, you protect yourself from real accountability.

The cost

There is, however, a tremendous cost to leading with a Victim mindset.

Too much potential for change, innovation and impact is stymied when Victim is in residence. Teams doing important work get derailed by this mindset. People get disillusioned. Cynical. Defeated. Over time this can become entrenched as the standard way of working and relating.

There is less opportunity to solve complex problems with a Victim mindset. If we believe 'I can't, and nothing I do will matter,' then the resourcefulness and energy needed to tackle the many challenges we face will be missing. This mindset is also fed by the way these issues are framed – that they are too big and too significant for a person to have any impact. It gets underlined through our social media feeds and the news at large, which focuses on negativity and fans overwhelm.

The lie that feels true at the heart of the Victim mindset is that 'I am not enough, and can never be enough to overcome the challenges I face'.

When we think we can't make a difference or impact a situation, or when we give over our power to something outside ourselves – we forfeit access to agency, ingenuity and control. This is the least effective leadership quadrant. Yet this mindset too can be changed.

> The lie that feels true at the heart of the Victim mindset is that 'I am not enough, and can never be enough to overcome the challenges I face'.

Shifting from the Victim mindset

Life is sometimes tough. Pandemics happen. Health issues lay us low. Relationships flounder. Hits to the bottom line create anxiety. Yet the Victim mindset need not be your only recourse, even when surrounded by chaos. The prospect of being a *lead in* leader can feel far removed when you are caught up in Victim. However, working through the quadrant axes gives pointers to shift into the top right quadrant of a Leader's mindset.

Victim mindset is bound by the fixed/limited axes, so its antidote is found in the growth/expansive distinctions. When stuck in Victim, look to the fixed mindsets that grip you most. It might be that you believe you can't change. You're just not capable. Or you believe there is nothing you can do. Find the most useful growth mindsets to cultivate. Nurture those that offer a more empowering perspective. Remember that these beliefs are not you. You can change them.

Now look to which limited mindsets are highest for you. Are you stuck in a loop about the past, believing that, despite efforts, nothing can improve the situation? Look for the expanded mindset that offers a different way to view your predicament. It might be reframing the past and seeing that your failures don't define you. They aren't you. They offer information on what you have tried before, but the future is still unwritten. It is there to be created.

The Delayer mindset

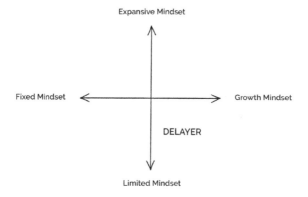

Figure 6: The Delayer mindset

The bottom right quadrant is where we find the Delayer mindset. This combination of fixed and expansive mindsets can see people procrastinating and putting off actions and decisions. Think of it like driving a car with one foot on the accelerator (expansive) and the other on the brake (fixed). You want to go forward because you see things are possible, but...not now, I'm not ready, we can't do that yet.

With the Delayer mindset, you want something to happen, and you know it can, but you just need a bit more preparation, or a boost in confidence, or extra data, and then you will make your move.

I find this mindset particularly common in those on the brink of going for a promotion or wanting to start something new. Delayer shows up when you think you should get an MBA before you apply for that incredible role, even though you have fifteen solid years of executive leadership under your belt.

Delayer mindset has a 'this before that' quality to it.

Delayer mindset has a 'this before that' quality to it. You have a dream, but you need more *something* before you can step into it. Take Amelia, who talked for ages about opening an art studio, but felt she needed to enrol in yet another art curation program. Or Fayola, who wanted to launch her online interior design business, but put off doing so because 'I should wait till the kids are older'.

Delayer mindset is different from prudently pausing before launching into something, but it's a fine line if this is your default. I know because, under pressure, this is mine! I can procrastinate and delay, not committing myself to a path of action or perhaps promising to do it later.

As a CEO, I was assertive and proactive, but I developed a way of buffering decisions – a classic Delayer tactic. Many years ago, I had a real wake-up about this mindset. My COO challenged me, saying, 'Do you know that when things are put to you, you often say no?' I was shocked. In my mind, I was a yes person, a 'Let's do this,' and a 'We've got this' person! A person of possibility! Yet that was sometimes not my COO's experience of me.

I thought about what she had courageously shared, and examined how I was showing up like that. On reflection, my 'no' wasn't that of the Dictator. It was a Delayer move – giving me space to decide. In my mind, it wasn't actually a 'no', it was a 'not now'. I didn't know how to ask for space to think, so instead, I put off decisions. In delaying this way, I stifled and blocked the leadership of people I was committed to empowering.

Procrastination

Procrastination – putting something off, even when it's important – is part of the Delayer's repertoire. Péng, an engineer working in a software company, struggled to finish his reports on time. It was torture for him. The problem was that it impacted his boss' perception of his performance. She was looking to promote someone from her team and thought Péng had the ability, except that his consistently late reports meant she couldn't respond properly to head office. His actions made it look like she didn't have a handle on things.

Procrastination and delay have two competing forces at work – the effort and sacrifice it takes to get something done, versus the gratification of an immediate reward. In Péng's case, the perceived slog of doing reports contrasted with the pleasure of doing almost anything else.

Leading with the Delayer mindset isn't about doing nothing. You can be very busy – but not focused on what's important, meaningful or necessary. Putting off dating until you've lost weight is a Delayer move. Not investing in the training you need because of the time it will take is classic Delayer. How many of us have cleaned the fridge and sorted out the kitchen drawers instead of addressing something essential in work or life? Spending weeks and months fine-tuning your strategy instead of launching a pilot? Designing your program and all the collateral before you've spoken to your market? Researching the best gym shoes and water bottles instead of exercising? All Delayer moves.

> You can be very busy – but not focused on what's important, meaningful or necessary.

Activity is happening, but not the kind that will propel you forward. With Delayer you are in the boat hugging the shoreline, and, as André Gide observed, 'You cannot discover new oceans unless you have the courage to lose sight of the shore.'

The benefits of the Delayer mindset include:

- Putting off feedback or results you think might be unfavourable to give you some reprieve

- Putting off difficult decisions or activities until later (so doing something else with your time)

- Avoiding the criticism that comes when you put yourself out there

- Feeling like you're doing something, even when you're not.

The costs can be high

Indecisiveness is a cost the Delayer pays by putting off what needs to be done. Energy spent filling up that space could have been directed towards something more useful. As the Himalayan explorer W. H. Murray wrote, 'Until one is committed, there is hesitancy, the chance to draw back, always ineffectiveness.'[20] Delayers fear this commitment. It locks them in, yet only by committing can the dream be initiated and then realised.

Delayers feel frustrated. The stop/go contradiction creates pent up energy. You know what you want, yet you don't go for it. The need to stay safe is at war with your ambition and aspirations. This frustration gets internalised when you tell yourself you're lazy or incompetent. But you're not.

Frustration isn't a one-way street, it's not a cost you bear alone. As shared earlier, this mindset negatively impacts others: people waiting for your input to further their part of the project; staff waiting for the decision to know what to execute; colleagues feeling disrespected and ignored by your lack of response. It can impact your career as well. Péng's Delayer mindset made his boss look bad, she hesitated to promote him.

You hold back – not just in the timing but in the idea itself.

Delaying dilutes your impact. That hesitancy can diminish the power of your idea. You hold back – not just in the timing but in the idea itself. Second-guessing means you don't back yourself. You may never experience the fulfilment and satisfaction of achieving what you want to achieve.

Where Dictators say 'This is what you'll do', and Victims say 'I don't know what to do', the Delayer mindset says, 'I might do this... later'.

Shift from Delayer to Leader

To move from Delayer, notice that you have access to growth mindset capabilities. Which do you want to emphasise to get you moving? It might be prioritising learning and new opportunities instead of being immobilised over potential failure. It might be recognising that applying effort and practice over the long term is normal – you don't have to have it mastered to begin.

Now identify the limited mindsets holding you back. These might be believing you can't lead, or you don't yet have enough of something (skill, training, time) to start your venture. This is a version of the scarcity mindset that we devote Chapter Seven to. Now choose a relevant expansive mindset to get you unstuck.

If you are blocked by perceived limitations ('I can't do this because I have to do that'), consider how you might reframe them. My neighbour Steph wanted to help out at an animal welfare organisation but hesitated, thinking, 'They probably won't want me as I'm not a vet'. She caught this Delayer tactic and realised that while she had no control over whether they would want her, she did have control over putting herself forward and seeing what might happen. Steph took her foot off the brake and got herself out of Delayer. As it turned out, she didn't need prior skills – they taught everything in-house. Steph is now a volunteer wildlife carer for koalas, and she looks after them every Monday afternoon.

Default mindsets are not who you are

These default, unexamined mindsets of leading – Dictator, Victim and Delayer – are not your personality. They are not you. You might be so attuned to them that they feel like they are you, but this is not so.

Leading powerfully is as available to you as it is to anyone else.

For example, perhaps you've had a few knocks that have dimmed your confidence, so when a colleague misunderstands you, or you're not included in key meetings, you are triggered into a Victim mindset. But this is not who you are, even if it has been a constant pattern since childhood. Leading powerfully is as available to you as it is to anyone else. To think otherwise is to believe that our past is the blueprint for our future.

The same is true for Dictator and Delayer. As a default Delayer, I used to wonder whether this behaviour was at some level my true nature. Once when particularly in the grip of that mindset, I tried justifying it through astrology. (We Librans are famed for hesitating and not making decisions.) And what a Delayer move that was – searching the internet for astrology interpretations instead of just getting on with it!

Others feel similarly about leading as a Dictator, thinking this is 'just me, it's who I am'. Well, no. They are mistaking Dictator and autocratic behaviour for an outdated concept of 'being decisive'. Being domineering is not who you are. You've just internalised old tropes about leadership and made them your own.

Context is everything

If you're still on the fence that maybe your leadership style is really your personality and who you are, consider this. Even with your preferred default mindset, you can drop into any of the others – at any time. That's because different contexts elicit different responses. When working with your boss, or head office, you might find yourself coming from a Victim mindset. You feel misunderstood and unappreciated. 'If only they knew what it was like here on the ground. They are completely unreasonable.'

> That's because different contexts
> elicit different responses.

Then, with your direct reports, you might be most often in the Dictator space, where you rarely listen, with a one-way communication style that tells them what you want, when you want it, and how you want it done.

And then, with personal ambitions, you Delay. Whether exercising or starting that side hustle, you put it off. You want to do it, but you delay taking action.

Three mindsets in one day.

Whichever mindset you find yourself in, it is always possible to *lead in*. You can move into the Leader's mindset quadrant at any time, in any circumstance. You are not fated to lead in old, unsatisfying ways. We'll explore this further in the next chapter.

Key points

- Default ways of leading sit at the intersections of growth and fixed, limited and expansive mindsets. These indicate how you behave in that quadrant and give the necessary focus to access a Leader's mindset.

- Mindsets give rise to behaviours. Yet what gives rise to mindsets is often contextual. Different contexts elicit different responses.

- Each default mindset has its benefits as well as its issues. All work to a certain degree – that's why we reach for them – they become an unconscious go-to. Seeing what the mindset costs us can push us to develop a Leader's mindset.

Questions to consider

- What is my default leading style?

- What conditions or events trigger it?

- What do I gain from leading this way when under pressure?

- How is this not working for me or others?

- What is one thing from the growth or expansive mindset axis that I can practise this week to begin to *lead in*?

Five

The Leader's Mindset

To *lead in,* you must apply the Leader's mindset. When you do, you are in the ultimate results zone. This is the mindset that cuts through obstacles and blockages. With it, you lead yourself and others with clarity, empathy and action.

The Leader's mindset is found in the upper right quadrant, where growth (continual improvement) meets expansive (seeing that things are possible).

I love the Leader's mindset because it is inclusive and accessible. It is not related to a job title, nor does it require others to follow you. Everyone can lead with this mindset – whatever your age, position or history.

This mindset is not easy, though, and it is rare to master it without conscious thought. We must choose and practise it, and like a muscle that gets stronger over time, it is worth the effort. The Leaders' mindset is evident in the extraordinary things people have done, where focus, grit, heart and hope were needed.

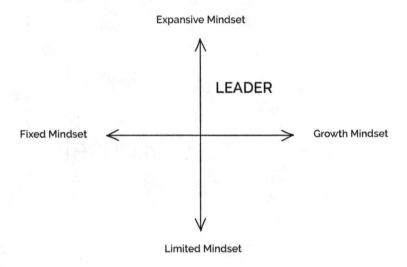

Figure 7: The Leader's mindset

The Leader's mindset

Essential to this mindset is knowing that you are not at the mercy of circumstances. Yes, stuff happens that is often out of your control. Yet how you respond and adapt is always up to you. Lesser leaders seek clues from external variables, which determine how they show up. When operating with a Leader's mindset, you decide how you show up, circumstances notwithstanding. You don't wait for fairer winds before setting your course.

The Leader's mindset is especially needed now. The challenges facing us are immense, and our default mindsets are not up to the task.

They bog us down in hopelessness and despair, and by staying there, we take ourselves out of the game.

I get it. I, too, can veer between defeat and fury when I see what passes for leadership and the consequences that come from it. Yet falling to a Victim mindset helps no one, and neither does Delaying. Being a Dictator, even for the right cause, will alienate more than you will achieve.

We need new ways to stand in the cauldron of confusion, pain and fear that modern life can provoke, without it burning us out. We need to access power that is collective, personal and transformative. To me, this is available with the Leader's mindset.

> We need new ways to stand in the cauldron of confusion, pain and fear that modern life can provoke, without it burning us out.

The Leader's mindset isn't a rigid, know-it-all approach to getting stuff done. Quite the opposite. It requires a connection to self and to what makes us human. It requires humility and vulnerability, authenticity and courage.

Yet, a Leader's mindset is not naïve. You accept that you will face difficulties and obstructions when working on anything worthwhile. That means you don't waste energy railing against the inevitable blocks and disruption. You know that the structural constraints, limiting beliefs, and personal insecurities which keep us small can be transformed, and you lead from that place.

This mindset is paradoxical because it is both intensely personal and communal. Personal because you need to choose it moment by moment, but communal because you know that sustainable change cannot happen alone. You need others. When you *lead in* with a Leader's mindset, you take responsibility for how you show up, and you build a movement of leaders.

A Leader's mindset doesn't waste time fighting reality or going into drama. You don't moan to others or pick up your bat and ball to go home, even when the odds are against you. Instead, you stay in the arena and step up with the optimum response. You do not get derailed: you know that even if the outcome is uncertain (which it often is), it's never over until the final whistle blows. And even then, you know that something else can rise from the ashes. You have learned lessons and fought hard for the wisdom that will carry you to your next initiative. You know that nothing is ever truly lost.

With a Leader's mindset, you remind us all of who we might be.

You are activated in your leadership and inspired to work for a future worth creating when you *lead in*. You have a clarity of purpose that is an invitation for others – not a demand. With a Leader's mindset, you remind us all of who we might be.

You can activate your Leader's mindset when challenges arise. Perhaps a client you expected to sign pulls out, or a team member you need isn't available because of other priorities. A non-Leader's mindset panics and feels disempowered. Their thoughts immediately go to 'Why is this happening?' or 'How could they let me down?', both reactions typical of fixed and limited mindsets.

Instead of falling into that trap, the Leader's mindset understands that you can choose the best possible response even under unfavourable circumstances. From the examples above, that might mean carefully analysing the client's decision, and from this learning what you can. It could mean getting up to speed when a colleague is unavailable, rather than being stuck in frustration and resentment. When you *lead in*, you respond to what is needed now. Rather than lose focus, you take the best possible action to keep moving toward your goals.

Who is a leader?

Leadership is available to everyone, and owning this can unleash significant breakthroughs. I learned this truth from women in villages who live this daily. They *lead in*, and in doing so, achieve incredible results. If you are wondering whether you could be this kind of leader, consider this research from Bangladesh.

In December 2019, I surveyed more than six hundred village women trained as community leaders. These women were part of the Unleashed Women Leader's Network, a national volunteer group of more than nine thousand women. They were trained by The Hunger Project to activate leadership mindsets, mobilise their communities, and take actions to tackle the entrenched issues women faced. These issues included access to safe drinking water, stopping child marriage, ensuring children attended school, and stopping the endemic violence against women in many households. These women were united by a vision that each home and family would be safe and fed, with good health, access to services, and opportunities for income generation. They were committed to solving challenges that had been with the people for centuries.

Through the survey, I wanted to understand how each woman viewed her leadership ability before and after The Hunger Project's interventions. I wanted to know how (and even if) they saw themselves as leaders. The sample was diverse and included women from different parts of the country and different educational standards. About ten per cent of the women surveyed were not literate, so they answered the questions orally to volunteers who captured their responses. The questions were based on a rating between one (lowest) and ten (highest).

They were asked, 'How would you rate yourself as a leader before and after The Hunger Project?' Of those women surveyed, 301 out of 638 (47%), rated their leadership ability between one and three (on a scale of ten) before any training. This number changed significantly after the training when only 32 women (3%) still rated their leadership ability as low.

How would you rate yourself as a leader
before and *after* being trained?

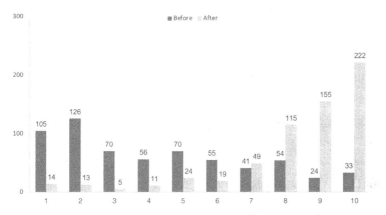

This graph shows how 638 women rated themselves a score out of 10 as a leader before and after
participating in The Hunger Project trainings. Surveyed December 2019, Dhaka Bangladesh

Figure 8: The Hunger Project training evaluation results

At the higher end of the continuum, 111 women (17%) rated their
leadership ability between eight and ten before any training. These women
were already in action, standing up for the rights of their community.
Yet after leadership development, this number jumped to 492 women
(78%). This is a clear example of how a limited mindset about your
ability to lead can change with the right kind of intervention. This shift
in perception activated the women in a way they hadn't thought possible
and led to tangible benefits.

Consider these stunning achievements by women who initially
thought they weren't leaders or had little leadership ability. Between
July 2017 and June 2019, the Unleashed Network collectively stopped
3,521 child marriages, oversaw 3,666 safe deliveries, and ran 17,676
separate campaigns on child marriage, sanitation, nutrition and dowry.
It's a remarkable example of what's possible when we *lead in*. It's also

a sobering tale about the waste of human capacity when old limiting attitudes about leadership and who wields it locks out women like these, who have made such a contribution.

Shouty wavy people

Twenty-two-year old Rejbina Akter could have been one of those women locked out of expressing her leadership potential. Rejbina is a leader and sees herself as such, having made much progress in her small village to encourage parents to send their daughters to school. She said that before being trained about mindsets, she did not think she could lead. She could not ever be a leader because, for her, a leader was 'someone who shouts and waves his hands around a lot'. (I really loved this. I could picture it immediately.)

Let's break it down, as I think it says a lot about what many of us believe about leadership.

'A leader shouts a lot.' Shouting denotes dominance. It's raising your voice to override other people to make a point. It's taking all the oxygen in meetings and not letting others share their views. Shouting is megaphone communication.

'A leader waves his hands around a lot.' This doesn't have to be literal, but it reflects people in leadership positions who take up space and demand attention. Maybe they don't hand-wave a lot, but they create drama and use it to get what they want.

That last part of Rejbina's comment referred to someone who waves 'his' hands around. Unfortunately, this view of leadership as a man's domain is internalised and reinforced in our cultural, political and work environments. It's easy to count yourself out when this is all you see, and they are not like you.

A leader's mindset was activated within Rejbina and the other members of the Unleashed Women Leaders network. For the first time, they could create and imagine a style of leadership most appropriate for them. They didn't just copy what they thought leaders 'should' do. They led and influenced in a way that suited them. Some women did so through small hut meetings, preferring a one-on-one approach. Others led larger village meetings, helping their community take action to end hunger. Some stood for politics. Others worked with youth to run campaigns to stop child marriages. With every person, leadership expression was uniquely and powerfully their own.

When we move out of a paradigm that leadership needs to look a certain way, we can reimagine what it might look like for each of us. When we *lead in*, we can invent our own version.

Enrolling others for maximum impact

A Leader's mindset inspires others to act. You know what you stand for, and you become the standard upon which you uphold. You don't entertain behaviours, words or attitudes that undermine that. This is not just relevant for senior managers. Junior members and new recruits can hold firm to their ideals and support others to do the same.

A Leader's mindset
inspires others to act.

Some years ago, an intern at my organisation attended a meeting with some donors. She overheard one speak disparagingly about climate change and how it was all a beat-up, and this disturbed her. Knowing that climate change is a huge issue for people in sub-Saharan Africa, she came to me with her concerns. I was grateful and met with the donor for a robust discussion. While he didn't change his stance about climate change, he did agree not to disparage The Hunger Project's commitment and work in this area. I informed the intern and thanked her for coming forward.

Sometimes speaking out is more problematic, but that doesn't mean you can't *lead in*. You always get to choose how you show up. It might require a private conversation with an out-of-tune colleague. Or you might need to rethink your approach.

Sofía is a software engineer from Colombia who works at a large tech firm in North America. She was frustrated that women from Latin America were overlooked and marginalised at her work, especially since the corporate mandate was to attract and promote women. She had presented to her leadership team about this and put together plans to support the promotion of other Latinas. Sofía had come to a stop, fearing she was not making the headway she hoped for, and she was experiencing pushback from her superiors. She also worried her advocacy in this area was marking her as an annoyance and would stall her from progressing further in her own career.

Scenarios like Sofía's are common, so what difference can a Leader's mindset make? In Sofía's case, a lot. She realised she was trying to make inroads for Latina women on her own. It was an area she was passionate about, but it meant she could be sidelined. Instead, she reached out to colleagues to form a broader wedge to make progress. Her vision was clear and inspiring – she now asked other people to hold and spread the message. It became not just Sofía's initiative but one that others were also committed to. In *leading in* with a Leader's mindset, Sofía increased her capacity for impact. Instead of letting her concerns stop her, she created a movement that was bigger than her. Sofia gained momentum on the issue within the company without drawing fire.

You uplift your team and hold them accountable for their results and impact.

We may see the new paradigm that *lead in* represents as overly warm and compassionate, full of people who don't really care about results. (At least this is what Dictators think!) However, this misconstrues what powerful, centred leadership is. When you *lead in*, you are not wishy-washy. Like the women in Bangladesh, you are committed to achieving your goals. You uplift your team and hold them accountable for their results and impact. You do this because you know they are capable when given the proper support and empowerment.

Leading from a Leader's mindset means:

- You can be in any part of the organisation. It's not about the title. Don't think you can't make an impact just because you don't have the positional authority. Millions of women in their villages had no authority, yet still accessed this mindset to lead their families out of hunger and poverty.

- You believe in the inherent ability of every person to lead – including yourself. You know you always have more to learn, but this doesn't mean you have to wait on the sidelines if something needs to be said or done.

- You don't have all the answers, and you're comfortable with that.

- You have a vision that lights you up. You want to make a difference and you can stand in the tension between the present reality and the possible future.

- You engage and include others to realise that future.

Creating and empowering people to *lead in* will energise and enliven your organisation.

Today organisations need to both re-engage staff and navigate the volatile external environment. Creating and empowering people to *lead in* will energise and enliven your organisation. Your mission comes alive. You multiply the capacities and potential of others. Energy that is normally dormant becomes available.

True leadership is rigorous and forthright. It demands accountability and effectiveness. When you run a team, a business or a mission with a Leader's mindset, you call others into their potential. You expect them to rise, and you support this to happen.

Key points

- To *lead in* requires a Leader's mindset.

- A Leader's mindset is available to all. It does not rely on position, title, authority or agreement. It is a mindset you can access and act from.

- You can't *lead in* – and deny that same ability in others. If you can make an impact, so can everyone else.

- A Leader's mindset keeps you grounded in the outcome you seek. You don't let unfortunate circumstances derail you.

Questions to consider

- Do you see yourself as a leader?

- How can you activate a Leader's mindset in your team?

- When you look at the world, where is the ache in your heart that you feel you can't impact?

- What could you do with a Leader's mindset?

- What is one thing you can do today to begin?

Six

The Mindset Process

So far, we've looked at what it means to *lead in* and the different mindsets that can get in our way. We've seen examples of how others used mindsets to *lead in* to change their situation and realise their potential.

But, I can hear you asking, *how* do I do it? How do I stop sabotaging myself and step into being the leader I could be? How do I move past this barrier that I just feel is there? How do I find the confidence to achieve my biggest dreams? How do I *lead in*?

Rest assured, that's what this chapter is about. I'll share the Four-Step Mindset Process, which will help you catch and transform the thoughts and behaviours holding you back. This powerful tool will assist you to grow and develop as a leader. It's now your turn to work through your specific blocks and build your *lead in* capability.

Head and heart

You don't just *think* your way through your fixed or limited mindsets; you also need to *feel* and *do*. This might be unexpected – after all, the word mindset contains the word mind. Yet, in my experience, real breakthroughs come when we are thinking clearly *and* open and vulnerable with our feelings. There can be pain attached to beliefs that hold us back. After all, we believe them for a reason, and addressing them can mean bringing our awareness to feelings and thoughts that are uncomfortable.

While you can easily change some mindsets with a new realisation, stuck behaviours and mental patterns that have hung around for a while require more effort. We need courage and heart to delve beneath the surface. To truly *lead in*, we need to be honest to see things in a new light.

The Mindset Process has four steps that are sequential and circular. Like an infinity loop, each flows from the other and informs the whole.

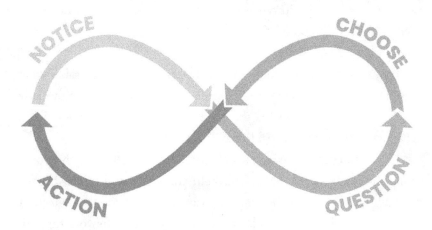

Figure 9: The Mindset Process

Noticing is the first step to identifying the frustrations and old stories we keep repeating that stop us reaching our goals. Noticing requires us to be present to what is going on – in both thought and feelings – and become aware of what we've made something mean. In doing so, we open to the possibility that the story we hold about ourselves, another person or a situation might not mean that at all.

Questioning deepens the process of unsticking ourselves from unhelpful beliefs. As you'll explore below, this encourages curiosity. It can also be a confronting part of the process because we find ourselves questioning long-held beliefs and stories – and sometimes even our identity.

Choosing provides an opportunity to break from unconscious reactions and choose how we want to show up. It offers the chance to forge a different path.

Action is where you demonstrate that choice. Taking action strengthens new mindsets and provides an opportunity for feedback and reflection.

In the Mindset Process, action is never the endpoint.

In the Mindset Process, action is never the endpoint. What we learn from being active in the world informs what we notice. We then question our assumptions, choose a new mindset, and take appropriate action towards our goal.

As T.S. Eliot wrote in *Little Gidding*,[21] 'We shall not cease from exploration, and the end of all our exploring will be to arrive where we started, and know the place for the first time'. The Mindset Process is a bit like that.

Notice

Noticing sounds simple, but it is not. We are good at reacting to what is in front of us, but it can be hard to recognise the mindset that gave rise to the reaction. You can't change what you don't observe. It's hard to do things differently when we are not aware of what we are thinking or telling ourselves.

Noticing can be tricky, as unhelpful mindsets can hide just out of sight – like a cyclist you don't see in your rear-view mirror. Noticing includes both thoughts and feelings. Tension and stress can signal that what you are dealing with is partly mindset.

Noticing is about being present to what's happening – the situation that is provoking your reactions, the story you're telling about it and the frustrations or feelings you have as a result. You get to see the belief that triggers your actions and responses.

Leading defensively

Amy is head of communications at a mid-tier consulting firm. She knows her stuff, her colleagues appreciate her, and she enjoys a positive reputation. However, each month Amy reports to a group of partners, which sends her into a real spin. She is stressed in the leadup, and during the meeting she feels second-guessed and criticised. Amy often emerges battle-scarred and misunderstood. Her work buddies agree that the partners are tough, so she garners sympathy and validation.

We talked through Amy's situation and the idea that while she can't change the partners, she can control her reaction to them in the meeting. I asked her to notice what she said about them, herself and the situation before, during and after each meeting.

Doing so was illuminating for Amy. She realised that she went into the meetings all armoured up as if she was going into battle. This mindset was there before she even stepped into the room! Everything she heard from that point on confirmed her view. Whenever the senior partner opened his mouth, Amy noticed she knew exactly what he would say, and she always gave it the worst interpretation. She felt defensive and attacked and would bristle and tense up when she didn't get the feedback she felt her ideas and position warranted.

When observing herself in action, Amy realised she carried an expectation of upset and provocation before anyone even spoke. She could see that her behaviour was a reaction to what she perceived, not what was actually said. In going into these meetings, defensive and closed off, Amy was never fully present to what was occurring. It hobbled her ability to show up powerfully and at ease.

That is why noticing is so important. It cuts through the morass of our stories and feelings and gets to the heart of what we make things mean. Noticing isn't about judging the conditions. Amy has little control over what the partners do or whether their manner is brusque or welcoming. She may absolutely have a prickly group of people on her hands. Noticing isn't about whether this is true or not. It is about observing how *you* react or respond. Typically, we overly focus on the situation, the dynamic, or the people we feel are causing it. This is leading out. Noticing is purely concerned with how you are showing up in response to whatever is going on.

Noticing allows you to see what is happening when you are not filtering through your limiting beliefs. It is the courage to recognise that while your situation might be difficult, your lack of power is not due to your circumstances – it's your mindset. Amy stopped giving so much energy to her opinions about the partners and focused more on showing up as the competent professional she is. This included noticing when she was reacting and consciously pulling herself back into her alignment and power.

> # Noticing is purely concerned with how you are showing up in response to whatever is going on.

It takes leadership to do this. You lose potency when you are at the mercy of events or conditions (or the partners in Amy's case). Once you view your reactions as a mindset, you can finally start to take your response into your own hands. You *lead in*.

Noticing feelings, thoughts and actions

If you notice constriction and stress, it might be your mindset. If you're feeling irritated, annoyed, defensive, cynical, apathetic or frustrated, it might have less to do with your conditions and more to do with how you are relating to them. Feelings are a great first indicator – like a canary in the coal mine.

Thoughts are also a powerful indicator that your mindset might be the blocker. Catch when you're judging someone or judging yourself ('They're so stupid' or 'I'm pathetic'). Notice when you are getting caught in old stories of how things didn't work, thinking, 'Of course they are like that!' or 'It's not my fault!'. It can be hard to do this because sometimes people are annoying, or the situation feels insurmountable. The point is to notice your mindset and the belief around it.

Behaviours are another way to catch mindsets. Notice when you're putting things off or acting in ways that you're not proud of, such as not listening, speaking over the top of people, or gossiping. Watch for things you are committed to but don't do. It's freeing to realise that maybe it's not because you are lazy or unreliable – but rather, it's your mindset.

How to notice

It's time to turn the spotlight on you.

You don't have to be a Zen monk to get good at noticing, although it does get easier with practice.

To help you figure out which mindsets are keeping you stuck, I'll suggest some sentences to complete that will help you notice. These have been useful for the thousands of people I've trained. There are a few ways to slice and dice this, so don't worry if the mindset doesn't pop right away. In fact, notice if you are now worried that the Mindset Process won't work for you. Well done! That's a mindset! This step of the process can be as simple as that.

(Note: For this process, pick just one limiting mindset to explore, don't jump around with a few. Use the same one through the whole Mindset Process in this chapter. You can repeat it many times for different limiting mindsets.)

Let's begin.

Write down what you want to be, do or have that is an aspiration or desire. Something you would like to accomplish or achieve.

_____

_____

Next, follow with your reasoning why you can't attain what you want. These are the obstacles you see, or the story you have about why it is hard for you, or unlikely, or impossible to achieve your goal. Don't overthink it – go with the flow and see what is there.

_____

_____

Now join the two together.

_____

_____

_____

Your sentences might look like this.

- 'I'd like to open up an online shop, *but I can't because I'm too old.*'

- 'I want to do something special for my friend, *but I don't have any money.*'

While it feels the part in italics is a reasonable justification, the purpose of this is to start to notice the story you automatically add that is blocking you from accomplishing your aim.

Now using the obstacle or scenario keeping you stuck, play with the following statements to help you surface hidden mindsets. See which one resonates most.

- I'd like to _____, but _____

- I need to be _____, before I can _____

- If only I had _____, then I could _____

- If only I could _____, then I would _____
- I'll never _____, because _____
- When _____ , I can be more _____
- Because (of) _____ , _____ will never change

I used the first statement to uncover why I was not writing. I was part-way through my first book, *Unlikely Leaders: Lessons in Leadership from the Village Classroom*, and I was stuck. I tried lots of tips and tricks to get going again. I berated myself, telling myself I was just being lazy and not committed. (Which was nonsensical because, at the time, I was running an organisation and was definitely not lazy. But mindsets, hey!)

Then I thought that perhaps I needed better time management to finish the book. Again, this wasn't really the problem, as I did know how to manage my time very well. I was stumped, stalled in a sea of frustration, self-criticism and inaction. I was trying to solve the problem of not writing by fixing something about me, trying to be better. Ironically, I wasn't attending to my mindset.

Once I realised this, I took my own medicine and wrote out my statements. (The writing part is essential – it circumvents the 'smart rat' part of the brain that has this all figured out and allows space for the unconscious to come through.)

I wrote the following: 'I really want to write a good book, but ... *that only happens to other people.*' This realisation floored me. I didn't realise I had this mindset, but I knew it to be true as soon as I wrote it. What shaped my inaction wasn't laziness or poor time management; it was the belief that I couldn't write a good book; only other people could. Noticing this mindset was the first step to finishing my book.

Some examples

- I'd like to work four days a week, but *I can't have that conversation with my manager.*

- *When I get my MBA,* then I can apply for more senior roles.

- Because of the downturn in the economy, *we will never meet our target.*

- *If only I could feel more confident,* I would start that business I've always dreamed of.

- *I need to be thinner* for someone to love me.

The mindset is the reasoning holding you back. It's the story you believe that keeps the unwanted situation in place.

You might notice that what usually follows a *but* or a *because* is a story, excuse, or justification for why you cannot have, be or do the thing you want to do, be or have. Uncoupling your situation from the unhelpful interpretation is the first part of noticing the mindset that keeps you stuck.

Here are some other mindset examples that people have found hold them back.

- I won't go for that promotion, even though I think I deserve it, *because I'll never be considered for it.*

- I'd like to meet someone, *but all the good ones are taken.*

- I'd like to start my business, *but I can't because of the kids.*

- Because of corruption, *we will never solve our community's issues.*

- Because we are short-staffed, *we will never make our project's deadline.*

In these examples, you can see that you are not disputing whether the conditions are true. You may have kids, and you may want to start a new business. You may live in a country with lots of corruption. I'm not asking you to judge or evaluate the conditions. In this step of the Mindset Process, you want to notice what you are making those conditions mean about your ability to lead. To make that impact. Get that job. Find that love. Change the world.

In this step of the Mindset Process, you want to notice what you are making those conditions mean about your ability to lead.

When I...

Here are some more sentences to try, this time starting with 'When I ...'

- When I _____ then I'll _____.

- *When I get more confident,* then I'll go for that new role.

- *When I lose five kilos,* then I'll feel good about myself.

- *When I get another degree,* then I can start selling my services.

- *When I find someone to share my life with,* then I'll be fulfilled.

These 'when I' mindsets have a 'this before that' quality. You can see how natural and sensible it sounds to link these. In the examples above, my fulfilment *does* require finding someone to love. Selling my services *does* require I get another qualification. Feeling good *does* require weight loss. That is how mindsets work.

Another way to find your hindering mindset is through 'need to be' statements. These include:

- I need to be _____ to have _____.

- *I need to be more experienced* before they will listen to me.

- I *need to be younger/older* to be respected.

Digging deeper

You're probably now noticing what happens when you link two separate ideas and make them one – they can become the 'truth' about how things are. You also probably noticed how getting to your limiting mindset took a few goes. That was Jess' experience too.

Jess is a mid-level executive at a large bank. She was short of her target when the rest of the team was smashing theirs, and she felt embarrassed and a bit ashamed. *What is wrong with me?* She went down the mental loop of how luck hadn't been on her side and 'if only' some things had been different. The further she was from her target, the more she tried different strategies – a classic 'lead out' move. But no matter what she did, she couldn't seem to get ahead. She even started sabotaging herself, wasting time online, and generally faffing about. She knew she was doing this but couldn't seem to stop.

Rather than try and fix her behaviour or create new sales strategies to meet her target, we focused on mindsets. And to get at the mindset underneath her lack of results, I asked her to write out her statements. She did, and they were:

- 'I'd like to make the target, but *it's now too late.'*

- 'I'd like to make the target, but *I've tried everything.'*

These were sort of yeah, like maybe, but she knew they weren't it. So she continued.

- 'I'd like to make the target, but *maybe I'm just not that great.'*

Yes – Jess really felt that one. She was getting at her mindset. I asked her to keep going and she wrote

- 'I'd like to make the target, but *I'm not capable.'*

Boom.

That was it. This was the mindset that underpinned Jess' relationship with results and drove her behaviour. If you really believe that underneath it all, 'I'm not that great,' or 'I'm not capable,' then struggling fits the narrative. You don't do what it takes to turn things around.

Mindset formula

Let's use Jess' example to explore a useful mindset formula.

$$\frac{\text{Event} + \text{Story}}{\text{Time}} = \text{Mindset}$$

There is the Event (as in what happened). This is Jess not making her target.

Then there is the Story (as in what you make it mean). This is Jess believing she'll never succeed; that she's not as good as other people. That there is something wrong with her.

Believed often enough over time, with enough supporting evidence for it to stick (real or imagined), it becomes Jess' mindset – *'I'm not capable. I'm just not that great.'*

If this mindset is left unchecked, Jess might even leave her role or drop out of her profession altogether. Or hide and fake her way through so no one notices just how 'not capable' she really is. (Jess did turn it around, as we shall see.) But without noticing the mindset at play, Jess was doomed to keep repeating her disempowered response to her situation. She was leading out and reacting to the conditions, not *leading in.*

As we'll discover in the next chapter, 'Maybe I'm not great/good enough' is a common limiting mindset. We have so much history and evidence to support it. 'I'm not good enough' goes back to childhood. Even saying it out loud can trigger feelings of vulnerability. The starting point for Jess was recognising that 'I'm just not that great' was a mindset and not the truth.

Jackie and Greg's mindsets

Jackie, a successful designer, shared that this first step of the Mindset Process ended up being all she needed. In catching the mindset, the obstacle popped, like a bubble:

'The first sentence I wrote was, "I'd like to create more, *but I don't have the time or emotional space."* I wrote some others that were in a similar vein. "I'd like to create more, but I can't with the kids / I don't have space with all the other demands I have." I kept digging in, and I realised that the actual sentence – my truth as I saw it – was "I'd like to create more, *but I'm not capable enough."* Wow. That hit me. I know I'm capable intellectually, but I can see that underneath everything, there is a belief that I'm just not. But now, sitting with it, my brain is going, "Oh my god, are you serious?" (She laughs.)' With this realisation, Jackie's block disappeared.

Noticing your mindset can bring up emotion.

Noticing your mindset can bring up emotion. You might confront the powerlessness you feel and the sadness around that. That's part of noticing too. Notice what comes up. Notice what meaning you attach to your belief. Notice the feelings.

Greg was concerned about his health and how his weight ballooned during the pandemic. Getting on top of his weight was a constant complaint and something he felt deeply resigned about. His first attempt at capturing the mindset was 'I'd like to get fit, but *it's just not possible in a pandemic*'. He realised immediately that this wasn't quite it, and a deeper limiting belief was at play. 'I'd like to get fit, but *I've tried everything. Nothing works.*' He noticed the profound truth this felt for him and the feelings of despair and hopelessness this bought up for him. (Don't worry, I didn't leave Greg hanging. We'll also get back to him in the next step!)

Organisational mindsets

Organisations have mindsets too, and the Mindset Process works for that. As we saw in the example of Microsoft in Chapter Two, culture and results can be torpedoed by the unexamined beliefs, identities and behaviours normalised in a team or business.

The CEO of an Australian FMCG business invited me to work with his leadership team. The business is more than a century old, with a proud track record of changing products and moving with the times. The business was in good shape, but the CEO was prescient enough to realise that it may not last another twenty years, let alone a hundred, without addressing mindsets. Longevity is no guarantee for sustained success in the current climate.

The leadership team unearthed some mindsets that were still running the show. A culture of busyness had become normalised – the answer to every 'How are you?' was 'Busy, got a lot on'. The team was inexperienced, with most new to leadership roles. That meant imposter mindsets, where people felt they were not good enough so constantly trying to prove themselves, were common.

The entire leadership team gathered for the first two days of a year-long engagement to develop *Lead In* leaders across the business. The first step was to surface shared organisational mindsets driving decisions. These included, 'We can't catch a break', 'We're busy, busy, busy', 'Wait – we have to see what the board says', 'I can't let my guard down', 'We're a friendly office so can't have tough conversations', 'Do what's expected and don't ask questions', and 'We're the little guys'.

Just noticing these and identifying shared assumptions and limiting beliefs gave the team language to articulate the unspoken norms shaping their behaviours. It laid the groundwork for the journey ahead to embed their soon to be chosen Leaders' mindsets.

Noticing has a power all of its own, and sometimes it is enough to see the mindset to change it, as it was for me with my book and Jackie with her space to create. But often, it's not, and that's ok. For now, it is enough to have distinguished the mindset holding you back from something important to you. We need to go to the next part of the

Mindset Process for those disempowering beliefs that feel totally, really, super-duper true.

Question

This next step takes courage – especially when we question beliefs linked to stories we've had running for a while. Here, we get to see that what we have told ourselves about a situation may not be the truth.

The power of questioning is that it gives us a chance to see the lenses through which we view the world. We get to take off those 'I can't do this' glasses or the 'it's not possible' glasses and get curious about them. Have a good look. Turn them around in your hands and find a new perspective.

Questioning a mindset takes leadership, and until we do so, we keep repeating the same patterns. Get inquisitive about what you are saying and believing. Is this belief supporting your leadership? Does it open up a new space of possibility? Does it help you grow or keep you stuck? Is it true?

The answer may be yes or no – it doesn't really matter. Just asking the question can lessen its grip. It gets you thinking about things differently. The belief has ruled up to this point because it went unquestioned. Considering that it may not be accurate starts a process of choosing how to respond and act.

In questioning the mindset, you are not questioning the reality of your situation. You are not asking whether it's true that you have a big mortgage you are struggling to pay, or a sick friend you are worried about, or long hours at work you can't seem to lessen. You are questioning what you make this mean about your relationship to this situation.

That is because this part of the process is not positive or magical thinking. It's not about denying your circumstances or trying to see them through rose coloured glasses. I would never question the conditions of a woman in an Ethiopian village. It is totally true that there is no fresh water, that the officials are corrupt, and the rains are late, and to suggest otherwise is disrespectful and verges on gaslighting.

This step is about questioning your power and agency in relation to those conditions.

This step is about questioning your power and agency in relation to those conditions. That's what you're exploring. You are checking whether what you've made your situation mean, about them, you or it, is true.

Your turn

Time to dig out the mindset you uncovered in the previous step and look at it differently. Go back to your sentence, and let's get curious about the meaning you've attached to it.

Some good questions I use include:

- Is it true?

- What's another way to think about this?

- What's really going on?

- Does this mean what I'm making it mean?

- What are the benefits of this belief?

- What is it costing me?

Let's look at these in relation to your mindset. We'll also see some examples of how other people used this step of questioning to help them *lead in*.

Is it true?

This is a great first question. Is what you are saying and believing even true?

Sometimes yes, and sometimes no. The point of this question isn't to land on a correct answer. Just look to see whether what you are saying and believing is true.

Remember Jess from the bank? Her mindset of '*I'm just not capable*' to achieve the target felt true to her – she was missing her targets when her colleagues were succeeding. That had to be the reason! To question this, Jess asked herself whether it was true that she wasn't capable. As a blanket statement, she recognised that '*I am not capable*' was false. Jess had experience and a track record in managing a team and producing results. So, if it wasn't true, what else was going on? How else might she think about this? She asked herself some great questions that opened up a new way of seeing things.

The questions that were most transformative for Jess assumed her capability. 'If I am capable, then what might be missing for me right now? What support do I need?' Doing so cut off the old story that 'I'm just not all that great'. Jess got curious about how she could succeed.

These questions pointed her to new ways to think about her goals and what steps to take to lift her sales results. It was a circuit breaker. It lifted her from her slump and opened her eyes to courses of action she couldn't see before when burdened by the old mindset. It reorientated her relationship with her colleagues and her customers. Jess didn't make that quarterly target, but she did end up the second most successful salesperson on her team when the annual results were calculated. Questioning her mindset made that possible.

The example of my writing block saw me notice my mindset of 'I can't write a good book *because that only happens to other people*'. When questioning it, I immediately saw that this just wasn't true because, at that stage, no one could possibly know whether it was going to be good or not! I would never know unless I wrote the book.

In asking, 'it that true?', I felt compassion for myself. I could immediately see the versions of this mindset that had swirled around me since childhood. As a child in a family that struggled, my history was seeing *other* people having lovely families and enough money to pay for the electricity bill. The mindset was that good things (like writing books) *happen to other people*. In questioning this, I could see the genesis of this mindset, and while I could empathise with younger me, I knew it was not the truth.

When we met Greg earlier, he was struggling with his weight and his mindset of '*I've tried everything to get fit, and nothing works*'. In questioning, he could see that wasn't true. When he fully considered it, he could see some things he hadn't tried and other approaches where he had cut corners. He hadn't fully committed and seen it through.

When questioning your mindset, you're not looking for a 'gotcha' moment to shame or berate yourself. You are freeing yourself from the habits of old thinking and patterns of behaviour predicated on mindsets that don't hold up.

What's really going on?

Sometimes it's helpful to ask what's going on. Often what we complain about on the surface is not really what's provoking our loss of power or energy. By asking, 'What's really going on?' you cut to the chase.

Often what we complain about on the surface is not really what's provoking our loss of power or energy.

Tom complained about his boss being disorganised, which made extra work for him. Tom's mindset was 'I work so hard, but *it doesn't seem to matter*'. He felt overwhelmed by the chaos and brought the issue to our mentoring session. Tom felt resentful and thought he might need to resign. In reflecting on what was happening and what he was making that mean about himself and his boss, Tom stumbled upon a profound insight. Something surprising sat at the heart of his frustration.

His dad was recovering from a stroke, and Tom was worried. He hadn't realised how bereft he felt about the little time they had spent together, and he was anxious his dad might pass away before he could see him. Tom hadn't fully recognised the depth of his concern; he had boxed the pain away, but it was still there. And that was what was really going on for him. The story about his boss' chaos melted – it hadn't been about that at all. Tom dropped his stress and annoyance about his work. He contacted his dad and committed to being there for him and letting him know how much he was loved.

'What's another way to think about this?' is another great question that gets us to examine the belief from different angles. Come up with a few different interpretations. 'Does this mean what I'm making it mean?' also allows us to stop and think.

What are the benefits of this mindset?

Every time I get stopped by a limiting mindset or fall into righteousness or complaint, I look to see how it is serving me. I encourage the teams and people I work with to do the same. That's because some of the most powerful questions to ask are 'What are the benefits of this mindset that is keeping me stuck in some way?' 'How is this mindset serving me?'

Some of the most powerful questions to ask are 'What are the benefits of this mindset that is keeping me stuck in some way?' 'How is this mindset serving me?'

Answering this question can cause a surprising reckoning. There's always a benefit to a limiting mindset. Always.

Living with complaints or excuses is not pleasant, but it works for us somehow. It gets us off the hook. We don't have to take responsibility. There's always a reason, a rationalisation, as to why we can't get past this. And at some level that suits us.

Not writing my book meant I never had to put it out for judgement and criticism. I didn't want the shame of facing people's assessment and finding myself wanting. I could keep pretending that I was writing but never face the panic and fear of opening night. This mindset kept me small and safe. I had thought not writing was about time management, but actually, it was about avoiding the risk of being seen and judged.

For Greg, the benefit of 'there's no point exercising or getting fit because I've tried everything and nothing works' was that he never had to do anything again! Go for a long walk? Why bother? Cut out calories, beef up exercise? Tried that. He ate what he liked and felt justified. Every time the scale didn't shift, he was vindicated. He also benefited because some of his friends were in the same boat, and as we know, misery loves company. He complained alongside them and felt like he fitted in.

Whatever mindset is holding us back does so because we collude with it. We hate it, yet we need it to prop up a smaller version of ourselves. Consider that the thing you complain about the most, the viewpoint you clutch tightly that doesn't empower you is there because it serves a purpose. When we start to see this, we can understand and empathise with why we sometimes struggle.

Naoki was on the leadership team for a global tech company based in Asia. He was frustrated by the constant demands from the head office in the US. He felt unappreciated and not in control of his work. 'No matter what I do, it won't make a difference. They don't listen or pay any attention.'

When Naoki noticed his mindset, he started to question it. He discovered how his feelings of frustration and impotency benefitted him. Naoki always had an excuse for not delivering his projects on time. He got to bitch and complain with his colleagues about the people in the US office, cementing a 'them versus us' sense of belonging. If the power lay outside his control, he didn't have to confront what leadership could look like for him – what he would need to say and risk. He kept himself safe.

Question your own limiting belief and explore what it offers you. If you are holding on to a story of 'I'm shy, so I get overlooked' – ask what the benefit is for you? It might be that you never have to step up to the court and face the ball. You can sit on the sidelines and criticise the play.

If you have a mindset of 'I would like to accomplish X but I don't have the time/money/energy,' consider how this benefits you. It can be hard to own, but even not having enough has an upside. If it's not enough time, you have an excuse for not elevating your skills or why the job wasn't finished on time. You stay in a 'small me' mindset when you feel you don't have enough.

If you have a mindset that 'I'd like to find love, but *all the good ones are taken*', you might benefit by not plunging yourself into the swirls and eddies of a relationship, with its inherent risks. Your life won't get messy. You can stand on that riverbank, dry but separate, contained in your own space.

Recognising the payoff that your limiting mindset brings is real leadership. It takes responsibility because in doing so, you are acknowledging that this mindset isn't happening *to* you. At some level, it works *for* you to keep it around. Interrogating this with an open heart can take courage. But it's where true growth lies.

What is it costing me?

This is possibly the hardest question to reconcile as we rarely confront it. Not writing my book was costing me self-expression. I knew I needed to share these stories of the women I had met through my work at The Hunger Project, as their voices and their lives were not being heard. I was making them even more invisible by not finishing the book.

What is the mindset you uncovered costing you?

Jeremy is an executive in a large consulting firm who struggled to reconcile his work commitments with spending time with his partner and two teenage children. Initially, this dichotomy showed up as a complaint, with him feeling like he was missing out and that his boss was being unreasonable.

In a mentoring session, he talked about wanting 'to be more present with my family when I get home, but I have so much work on its hard to do that'. Many people can relate to this. In our hyper-busy world, who wouldn't like to spend more time with loved ones, yet can't because of the demands? Yet, I was unsure that this was what was really going on for him. As we saw in the mindset formula, a clue that it might be his mindset was him linking 'not present with family' to 'so much work'.

By recognising this mindset, Jeremy realised that it wasn't about work. He desperately wanted to be more present with his family, but 'I don't know how to'. Noticing this moved him deeply.

When questioning his mindset, Jeremy confronted its benefits and costs. Underneath his struggle was a feeling of inadequacy. He didn't really know how to connect with his family, and he was embarrassed about that. He felt his daughters were more interested in their friends, so being on his phone, answering emails and having no boundaries around working in the evenings suited him somehow. It gave him a buffer. But at what cost!

Becoming present to the cost was very emotional for Jeremy. He was forfeiting precious time with his kids and missing out on guiding them and being there for them during their turbulent adolescent years. He was perpetuating old working male stereotypes that he did not believe in. He was not trusting the love and vulnerability in his heart and was warding off being rejected by those he loved the most. In getting clear about the cost, he was free to choose a different mindset and approach. The way became clear to manage work expectations in line with his deep commitment to his family.

Holding on to limiting mindsets does cost. The more we become present to them, the easier is our ability to choose a different mindset. When the cost of our smallness, complaints, and unfulfilled life becomes greater than the benefit of holding on to them, we can change. It takes courage, and few of us want to go there. On the surface, it seems easier to remain a victim, unwilling to grow, but we pay the price with our energy, satisfaction and impact.

Given this, now what?

One way to cut through an entrenched and difficult condition is to ask: 'Given this, now what?' Answering this necessitates radical acceptance of the present moment without changing or fixing it. Sometimes, things are tough, and no other way of looking at them will change that. No other interpretation cuts through. Asking, 'Given this, now what?' draws a line in the sand. It cuts off the story. It's a demarcation point that you can then build from.

Geetha lives in Madya Pradesh, India, in a small rural village where, in her words, 'the situation is very bad. The food the government sends for the school meals is coming late and of very poor quality. Our children are hungry.'

Initially, she believed 'there is nothing we can do. I can't do anything because I am a woman, and no one listens to me.'

For Geetha, the power of questioning wasn't about arguing the state of her village or the corruption that was causing school children to go hungry. The power came through questioning her conclusion: namely, that *I can't do anything, and nothing can be done*. That is mindset.

The cost of not acting was too great for Geetha to bear. Even though she is a woman with little education and low social standing, she asked herself, 'Given this is the situation I am in, now what?' In doing so, she put all the stories and beliefs from the past to one side. They were not relevant. For Geetha, the suffering in her community made her rethink who she was and what she could do. In doing so, she chose to *lead in*.

The power came through questioning her conclusion: namely, that *I can't do anything, and nothing can be done.* That is mindset.

Choose

Choosing is the third step of the Mindset Process, and it follows Notice and Question because when all is said and done, we each determine how we will respond, the action we will take, and what new future we will choose. At the heart of Choosing sits a little known truth. Even when we don't think we have a choice, we always do. Understanding this can be liberating.

Even when we don't think we have a choice, we always do.

The idea of having choices can sometimes feel like victim-blaming. You didn't choose to have asthma, be born into poverty, have that car accident, or live through a pandemic. However, we miss its transformative ability if we ignore the power of choice by only seeing it through this lens.

As leaders, we must accept that we always have a choice – even when the conditions are not favourable. We can't always choose what happens to us. But we can always choose how we respond, even if it's choosing how to show up in each moment.

Viktor Frankl wrote about this in his autobiography *Man's Search For Meaning*.[22] Imprisoned in a Nazi concentration camp, the guards had complete power over nearly every aspect of life. He had no choice of what he would eat, which work camp he was assigned or whether he got a blanket. Even whether he lived or not. They decided everything for him – except one thing – the freedom to choose his response to his situation. This freedom to choose is something we all have. Frankl wrote, 'Between stimulus and response, there is a space. In that space is our power to choose our response. In our response lies our growth and our freedom.'

This relates to mindset. The Mindset Process invites us to *notice* what we believe, think, or say. If we are not empowered by what we observe, we then *question* the assumptions. This helps us separate the story from the event. We then *choose* a new mindset for how we want to respond. We can choose to be loving. Forthright. Open. Trusting. Courageous. We can choose a mindset that gives us space to be our most powerful self, no matter the conditions.

So, what is choice? We usually think of it as a decision, having two or more things in front of us and needing to pick one, like a classic pros and cons list. In the context of the Mindset Process, choice means something more deliberate. Choosing isn't just about weighing up the options, looking at which we like best, or collating reasons about what's not good about the thing we reject. When we need reasons and justifications for our decisions, there is an element of making the other option wrong. Either way, it's always in relationship to something else. It doesn't stand alone.

Taking a stand

In this part of the Mindset Process, choosing isn't about making other options wrong and getting stuck in decision quicksand. Instead, think of choice as a stand you take rather than a decision you make. Taking a stand means holding to what is essential and what you believe is important. Archimedes, the Greek mathematician and inventor from 200BC, said, 'Give me a lever and a place to stand, and I will move the world'. Choosing has this same quality.

> Think of choice as a stand you take rather than a decision you make.

In his book *Essentialism*,[23] Greg McKeown writes, 'We often think of choice as a thing. But a choice is not a thing. Our options may be things, but a choice is an action. It is not just something we have but something we do.'

Choosing is about moving toward an empowered leadership stance without needing to have the reasons, proof or justifications in place. That is an important distinction because you can choose a new mindset that empowers you, irrespective of whether you think it will work, whether someone else has done it, or whether you have already tried it.

Choosing has an element of existentialism, which recognises that the individual is free and responsible for determining their own development, even with no certainty about the outcome. It becomes about making a stand for who you want to be and how you want to behave – in every moment. It's not based on the past, your belief, or other people's opinions.

Choosing is about moving toward an empowered leadership stance without all the reasons, proof or justifications in place.

It can be a real *aha!* moment because we are used to needing proof and evidence that something will be successful before choosing it. That gets us stuck in decision fatigue which choice circumvents. You can choose a new mindset, a new way of leading – moment by moment. You can experiment. Play with it. Be curious. Try it on. Develop mastery. With choosing, there is nothing to prove.

Once you have identified and questioned the mindset holding you back, it's time to choose a new one. Irrespective of circumstances, we each have the power to choose our mindset and choose one that gives us power and agency.

What new mindset will you choose?

There are hundreds, even thousands, to choose from. What's it going to be? Choose something that will empower you. All mindsets are made up. Even those that feel true and significant – you made it up! So you can make up another one that lifts your leadership and your life.

The FMCG company I mentioned earlier chose three mindsets to embrace: Champions of Possible, We Create, and Everyone Can Lead.

These became pillars of the company's culture. Across the business, people explored how they might lead with these mindsets at the fore. When a delicate client negotiation was in the balance, 'champions of possible' was activated. When team leaders were doing too much and not empowering their teams, 'everyone can lead' was invoked, with corresponding coaching and support. When the idea of setting up a new online outlet was raised, 'we create' helped them see how they could do this.

The CEO invested time and money to bring the whole organisation along with him and the leadership team. Change leaders were identified to help spread the word and embed these mindsets. These three mindsets became the platform for the company's expanded growth and inspired excitement for the future of the business.

Choosing a new mindset can feel strange at first, like putting on a new pair of shoes, but that doesn't make it false. Expect to walk around for a while before it feels comfortable.

Choosing a new mindset can feel strange at first, like putting on a new pair of shoes, but that doesn't make it false.

To move forward in writing my book, I chose the mindset that *I am a writer*. It gave me a whole new perspective. What does a writer do? She sits down to write. She publishes. She puts her thoughts and words out into the world. People read it. They comment.

Earlier, we met Naoki, who felt dominated by head office demands. He wanted to move beyond feeling resigned and cynical. Realising that railing against American management was a waste of his focus, he flipped his mindset to what he could control. Naoki noticed he was reactive and unresponsive about requests he thought were unfair. Instead of feeling annoyed, he focused on building relationships with his colleagues in the USA and breaking down his them/us thinking.

Naoki set aside the old mindset that he couldn't change anything and instead chose a new one, which was 'we are partners and on the same team'. This changed many things, including how he communicated with the US team, his boundaries, and how he negotiated last-minute requests. Over time, he recognised when he was reacting from his old mindset and could more quickly choose to lead from his new mindset. Even though he occasionally got annoyed and felt taken for granted, he mostly remembered to *lead in*.

Choosing to *lead in* takes courage. When Geetha faced the food shortage at the village school, she knew her old mindset of 'I can't make a difference. No one will listen to me,' wouldn't help those kids. When talking with other women in her community, it became clear that the school principal was redirecting the government-issued food to the black market and substituting it with rancid oil and lentils full of weevils.

Geetha went with other women to the police to lay corruption charges, and he was arrested. Hearing that the thugs with the stolen food were in the next town, the women went in a group to confront them. They seized the food and returned it to the school. Geetha then set up a roster for women to supervise the midday meals at the school, checking for food quality and clean preparation.

To achieve this, Geetha took on a new mindset of 'I can make a difference. I can change this. I can work with others to get our kids fed.' In doing so, she dropped the 'small me' identity and stepped into a larger view of herself. It opened her to possible risk. What if she wasn't successful? What if no one listened? What if the principal tried to threaten her? Even with these concerns, she knew the cost of inaction far outweighed the benefits.

It was moving to see the results of her incredible leadership. Geetha showed me the school lunches prepared with utmost care. The food was delicious and nutritious. It was inspiring to sit with the kids as they ate their hot meal and see the proud faces of the women supervising them.

Let go of the past

Choosing a new mindset means letting go of the past. It draws a line under it and says, 'Ok, what now?' It is an act of courage and compassion. It means letting go of the smaller you, the you that wants to stay safe or comfortable. Surprisingly, even anger, frustration, and despair become a source of comfort when you've lived with them for a long time. Saying goodbye to these old mindsets for a new possibility can feel upsetting and strange. And that's ok. That's part of the process. Every time you take a step in the direction of your growth, you say goodbye to that other you – the one that kept you contained, and you can do so with love and tenderness.

Surprisingly, even anger, frustration, and despair become a source of comfort when you've lived with them for a long time.

A new mindset opens up possibilities for different choices. Remember Jeremy? He struggled with not being available as a dad, so he chose a new mindset of 'I am a present and loving dad'. With this reframe, he showed up for his family in new and positive ways, from when he walked in the door after work to how he prioritised his work expectations.

He told me, 'In choosing to be a present and loving dad, I consciously get into that space when I get out of the car. I focus on where I am and my love for my family. When I walk in that door, I am there, not stuck in my head, back at the office. I seek the kids out. I focus on being loving and present and really being there for them. Sometimes I slip out of this mindset, especially when there's lots going on at work, or the kids are being dismissive, or if I'm just fed up and don't want to engage. I notice the pull toward putting on the tv or checking email and zoning out in those times. Then I ask – is this really how I want to spend my time? – and I choose again to be present. It's getting easier each time.'

Choice isn't a one-time thing, like a magic panacea.

As Jeremy shows, choice isn't a one-time thing, like a magic panacea. You don't just choose your mindset once and think that's done. When

142

you remember that the older, limiting mindsets have been with you for a long time, it makes sense that the new ones will need lots of practice. New mindsets are always bumping up against your old beliefs. Think of them like muscles. They need to be exercised.

Not positive thinking

Let's have a quick look at positive thinking because it can seem that choosing a new mindset is another version of that. Rest assured, it's not. Developing a Leader's mindset is very different.

Positive thinking tries to overlay rose coloured thoughts and forced cheerfulness on top of what's really going on for you. It over-emphasises naïvety and unrealistic optimism, especially when the situation doesn't warrant it. We do this because we want to feel better.

Whether trapped in a limiting mindset, facing a challenging situation, or feeling pain and anxiety, just wishing things to be positive without taking any action to produce a different outcome can reinforce resignation and despair. Operating over the top of difficult conditions with 'It's fine, all is great, I'm wonderful' isn't leadership. Rather than help you move forward, this will keep you stuck because, at some level, you still believe that things are most definitely not ok. If this is so, telling yourself otherwise won't make a difference.

Choosing to be realistically optimistic in the face of difficulties is not the same thing as positive thinking. Sustainable change can happen, but it takes doing the inner work, and processes like the Mindset Process can really help with this. Rather than wish away the troubles you face, you have the courage to deal with them. This is what it means to *lead in*.

Choosing to be realistically optimistic in the face of difficulties is not the same thing as positive thinking.

Not settling for positive thinking is challenging but ultimately freeing. Like pulling a thorn from your hand, there's tenderness and relief. Take off those rose-tinted goggles – they are not a source of power. Embrace instead what your frustration or wishful thinking is telling you, and use that to activate your power and agency. Get clear on what you want to do and who you want to be, and move forward from there.

Deep work

What's required of us now is deep work. With all that is happening in the world, confronting reality is hard. But if we don't it's very hard to get purchase. We are like worms wriggling on a hook. When we clearly see the situation and pause our story about it, we can choose to *lead in*.

This is key to tackling issues both personal and global. Notice what is concerning you without the stories of 'why is this happening, it shouldn't be this way, who's fault is this,' or your positive spin 'it's not so bad, I'm sure it will be fine, this is all for the best…'. Separating the event from the story – the 'what happened' from 'what we make it mean' gives us levers of mastery at our disposal. And this is the opposite of positive thinking.

I learned this when I first went into that village in Ethiopia in 1992 and saw the aftermath of famine. I saw sick children and women who had lived through too much. I saw crops failing to grow. I spoke to a woman who boiled stones in water, so her children thought their meal was nearly ready. No amount of positive thinking was ever going to improve that situation, and nor should it. I could have made myself feel better by thinking, 'Oh well, it's just these few villages and, you know, there's lots of really good other things happening in the world.' But that would have been inauthentic and denied reality. It would also have been untrue and deeply disrespectful.

Instead, I willingly traded my comfort and naïvety for actually making a difference. I owned the horror, and felt the grief and rage at the injustice, depth and deprivation of hunger - and used this to take action on behalf of a better future.

Confronting what was, and not my spin on it, changed everything.

Confronting what was, and not my spin on it, changed everything. I stepped up. I became a *lead in* leader.

Action

Determining and taking action is the final part of the Mindset Process. Realisations without a corresponding shift in behaviour remain meaningless insights. Once you have chosen your new mindset, consider the next best action you can take.

What action will you take that aligns with your new mindset?

If your new mindset is *'I don't shy away from difficult conversations'*, you might schedule a meeting with someone you have been avoiding.

If the new mindset is *'I make time for exercise'*, the action might be going for a walk, or booking a trainer, or having a conversation with your co-workers about the time you need to take for your physical wellbeing.

This fourth step in the Mindset Process is about deliberate, ongoing action.

Every new mindset must have an action attached to it. One that supports it to take hold. Be aware, though, of the pull to do something big and splashy; this is a real trap in our 'go big or go home' culture. This fourth step in the Mindset Process is about deliberate, ongoing action. It's about what you choose to do in this very moment. And the next. When starting a new mindset, don't let the largeness of the end goal derail your action. Smaller actions over time make the biggest difference.

Professor Teresa Amabile from Harvard University has written extensively on what she calls 'the progress principle', which sees taking small steps as a potent motivator.[24] Typically we underestimate the power of achieving something small. But for motivation, it's critical in encouraging us to continue toward the larger goal. Taking small action steps is especially true for retraining mindsets that have been in place for a long time.

If you want to find a life partner, and you've chosen a mindset of 'I am loveable', focus on small actions that help strengthen that mindset. Find a way to celebrate yourself by buying yourself flowers or spending time lying in the sun and enjoying its feel on your skin. Go on one date to have fun. Choose regular small actions that support your new mindset. Be gentle with yourself.

Your action might simply be to practice the first step of the Mindset Process and notice what's going on for you. Just notice. Bring your attention to what is happening in this moment and not the story you have about it. I find this useful before stepping into an important meeting or undertaking an activity I have some anxiety about. Simply noticing what I'm feeling and then choosing to bring myself into openness and calm makes a difference in how I show up. Practising this over time can have a profound accumulative effect. Remember, to *lead in* is not a one-off thing. You can choose it every moment of every day and take action from that perspective.

Choose regular small actions that support your new mindset.

Along with taking action, think about what support you might need to see it through. For Greg, who struggled with getting healthier, his new mindset became 'I'm committed to doing what it takes to get healthy'. His initial action was to walk around the block twice a day. It was a simple commitment, but there were still plenty of opportunities for his old resigned mindset to derail it. In thinking about the support he needed, he shared his commitment with his teenage daughter as a way of holding himself to account. The thought of her disappointment, if he didn't carry through, helped him develop this into a habit.

It can take courage to stick to the action that corresponds with your new mindset. Remember, there was a reason why the older, limiting one hung around – at some level, it was comfortable and worked for you. With your actions, normalise the discomfort. That doesn't mean it's not working; it means you are growing out of your zone of comfort.

Bringing the Mindset Process together

We had an above-ground, oval-shaped swimming pool in our backyard when we were kids. We loved to create a whirlpool effect where the water flowed around the pool in one direction, and we could float along with it. It needed many of us to walk in the same direction for quite some time to get to that point. It was hard going at first. The water was static but eventually, it started to swirl, and we would hop on our boogie boards and float around, like in a water park.

Changing your mindset so it sticks is like that. We are always up against some resistance. You may have chosen a new mindset, but your current ways of operating are calibrated to your old assumptions and beliefs.

I love author Steven Pressfield's idea of how this resistance works. In *The War of Art*,[25] he writes: 'Rule of thumb: The more important a call or action is to our soul's evolution, the more resistance we will feel toward pursuing it.' Limiting beliefs and mindsets (resistance) only rear their head when we want to elevate our life in some way. They don't bother us if we want to keep at a current or lower level than we are now. When we want to grow or achieve more, resistance kicks in, trying to hold us back.

When you start to challenge your old beliefs and mindsets, resistance strikes. It looks like excuses, justifications and complaints. There's always a reason why something can't happen – or at least not now. Resistance croons, but it is not your friend. Notice your mindset and then turn the blowtorch of rigorous questioning on it to see the story for what it is – a distraction. A device to keep you small, contained and unfulfilled. Pressfield again: 'Most of us have two lives: the life we live, and the unlived life within us. Between the two stands Resistance.' Or, as I see it, our limiting mindsets.

Before you take an important action, use the Mindset Process. Perhaps you have to call a client, and you're feeling nervous. Rather than just dial the number, spend a moment getting present and noticing where you are at. I do this through breathing. Even one long breath in and one long breath out brings me back to my body and the moment. I then choose to be light, focused, and open on the call.

I advise my clients to do something similar. Noticing when you're in reaction mode gives you a chance to choose another way of being. It might be by taking a few breaths before you make that call. It might be observing the tension in your body and then straightening and stretching. Or it may be feeling the slump of disempowerment that comes at you from left field, catching it, then transforming it.

That happened to me this morning. I woke up pumped and ready to rock and then read something online that triggered immediate feelings of futility. I noticed it instantly. Rather than give into 'small Cathy', I chose instead a version of me that is courageous and expansive, someone who is committed to doing the best she can. And with that, I went to work. The whole process took only a few moments.

Mindset work is a partnership between head and heart.

The first three steps of the Mindset Process – Notice, Question and Choose – are active, not passive. They require inner work and awareness that can be as strenuous as any action taken in our life. These first three steps activate our leadership, and the fourth step, Action, springboards us more powerfully into the world. You are clear, focused and intentional, ready to make your mark.

When you fall back into old mindsets, including Dictator, Victim or Delayer, know that this is part of the journey everyone travels. It doesn't mean you are a failure or that you'll lead like this forever. It means you are human, and this is normal. You are learning a new skill that will take time and practice. That is why the Mindset Process is like an infinity loop. We are always discovering new things. Always becoming. There is no end to our growth and understanding.

Key points

- The Mindset Process is a four-step approach to lovingly and rigorously identify the mindsets that get in our way and choose new ones that give us more power and agency.

- Examining mindsets takes leadership and courage. It's safer and more comfortable to stay in our old groove, even if it is unsatisfying. Understanding the benefits of staying stuck and the cost of not changing helps us move beyond our limiting beliefs.

- Mindset work is a partnership between head and heart. Your humanity is a beautiful, precious thing. For real change to happen, you can't shame or berate the old you. Your feelings and your thinking are co-equal guides.

Questions to consider

- What would I do now if I didn't have this limiting belief about myself? Who could I become?

- What would someone with a Leader's mindset do in this situation?

- What action can I take now that supports my new mindset?

Seven

The Scarcity Mindset

Hard-wired for lack

Scarcity is one of the most prevalent and pervasive limiting mindsets. It's the belief that we lack something important, and its absence is why we struggle, suffer and don't make progress.

Getting to grips with the scarcity mindset is essential for a leader who can cut through. Scarcity undermines and stalls great initiatives and projects. This mindset is so hardwired in us that we don't even notice it, and because it's similarly ingrained in others, they don't notice either. Everyone gets caught up in the turmoil of lack, scarcity, drama and fear. This is classic leading out – focusing on the circumstances. Instead, to *lead in*, you must recognise the mindset for what it is and work to create a space of possibility and momentum for yourself and others.

This chapter will dig into the scarcity mindset and explore how to get relief from it. When you transform your relationship to scarcity, you free up mental space and increase your impact.

I've devoted a whole chapter to this because scarcity thinking is at the root of many of the ways we get stuck. When we feel a lack, scarcity mindset is sitting right there underneath. Scarcity is a mindset of not enough of whatever we believe we need to survive and succeed – money, time, help, resources, people, love, food, friends, hope for the future, confidence – the list goes on!

When we feel a lack, scarcity mindset is sitting right there underneath.

Scarcity's universality makes it harder to distinguish as a mindset. When people around us talk about not doing something because they don't have the time or money, we don't question it. It correlates to our own life experience. It checks out.

The scarcity mindset is ubiquitous because it is not something we create – it's wired into society. As James Suzman writes in *Work: A History of How We Spend Our Time*,[26] 'our preoccupation with scarcity is a hangover from the early agricultural state some 12,000 years ago when we went from foragers to farmers.' In being able to cultivate and store food for the first time, Suzman argues humans homed in on the idea that we might run out – we might not have enough – and this fear of lack only increased during the agricultural and industrial revolutions.

In noticing and then transforming the scarcity mindset, we are up against two things; our personal stories and histories - and 12,000 years of evolution.

A day in the life of scarcity

Let's look at how mindlessly prevalent scarcity appears in a day. How much of the following can you relate to?

You wake and groan, 'I haven't had enough sleep'. As you run around getting organised to leave the house, you mutter, 'I don't have enough time'.

You're at a meeting, and a project is running late, and you worry, 'This timeframe is unrealistic. We'll never do it by then.' You need more people to be involved, but, 'I don't have the budget'. You need to delegate work to someone else, but you don't, because 'they lack finesse. They don't pay enough attention to detail to save me time.' You want to apply for a new role, but you fret, 'It will be a waste of effort. I won't get it. I don't have the experience.'

You plan to go to the gym, and you know you'll feel better afterwards, but you don't go, thinking. 'I need that time to finish my sales report.' You head home to cook dinner, but you don't have all the ingredients. 'Someone ate all the cheese, so I don't have everything the recipe calls for' – and you order takeaway. You read an article about climate change and you feel despairing, but you think 'I don't have connections that matter, or influence. We're running out of time and there's nothing I can do.' You try to put the feelings to one side but the anguish remains.

You're invited to a party and agonise about what to wear because 'I'm not thin enough'. You lie in bed at night stewing about your financial situation, 'I don't have any money' (or its twin 'I should have more money'). You look at the clock before dropping off to sleep and groan,

'It's so late, I won't get enough sleep.' And on it goes. This mindset is so exhausting and omnipresent that even typing this raised my stress levels!

We have all experienced scarcity thinking in some form. Imagine if we could loosen its grip on our lives. What might be possible? This chapter explores just that, using all aspects of the Mindset Process.

We have all experienced scarcity thinking in some form.

Untangling the scarcity mindset

Part of what makes the feeling of lack stay with us for so long is because scarcity feels like the truth.

It is true that *my sleep was interrupted / I only have $10 in my wallet / the team budget was just cut.* However, without thinking, we link the situation or event with what we make it mean, which then becomes the truth. As we know from the mindset formula, that's how mindsets are formed.

So while it's true that *my sleep was interrupted,* it does not then make it true that *I'm going to be terrible in that meeting.*

It may be true that *I only have $10 in my wallet,* but it does not make it true that *I'm poor and bad with money.*

It may be true that *the team budget was cut,* but this does not mean that *we can't achieve our goal.*

There are circumstances – and then there's what you make them mean.

When we don't know the Mindset Process, it can be hard to see these two things – the event and the story we attach to it – as unrelated. But they are, and the trick to getting unhooked from scarcity is recognising that the conditions do not cause the mindset. There are circumstances – and then there's what you make them mean.

External conditions

Scarcity is more closely linked to external conditions than other mindsets. It is instantly triggered by something that happens or a change in our environment, and the panic and worry quickly escalate. A client cancelling the job means we have to start staff layoffs immediately! A bad review for your product means no one will ever buy it again! Something happens, and hello, scarcity mindset!

Research supports that a change in circumstances triggers fear of loss. Nobel Prize winner Daniel Kahneman and Amos Tversky coined the phrase 'losses loom larger than gains' in their study on loss aversion, which shows that the psychological pain of losing is twice as powerful as the pleasure of gaining.[27]

That means when something happens, we are more likely to immediately see the worst outcome, even if that is the least likely scenario. We reach for the potential loss and its ramifications. We have to work much harder to see the upside when life throws us curveballs. This fuels the scarcity mindset.

What we think we lack might not be it

In an overworked world where long hours are normalised and time is scarce, it is vital to rethink what is essential and work differently. Sometimes what we think we lack (often time or money) isn't what is scarce. As we'll see below, lacking a compelling vision for your life can be the anchor that holds a scarcity mindset in place.

Ronnie works for a large multinational organisation and regularly clocks eighty hours a week on the job. She is a leader in her part of the business, and the scale of work keeps growing. Ronnie thought she had no choice about working such long hours – there was no other way to keep on top of a moving tsunami. She believed her organisation expected people to work this way and these hours were 'the way things are done around here'.

Her marriage was suffering, as was her health. Ronnie felt she was on a hamster wheel that she couldn't get off. I worked with her team to help them *lead in*, and this included individual mentoring with Ronnie and the executive team.

When Ronnie shared her long work week in our initial session, I was aware this was typical in her organisation, where everyone confessed to similar hours. There was lots of agreement for this: 'We have so much on, it's coming up to our biggest season, there's no other way I can get this done without putting in the mega hours.' Yet I wondered if it was true that there was not enough time? Was it true that 'I can only achieve my goals if I work eighty hours each week?'

I believed there was a scarcity mindset in play.

This mindset of believing there's not enough time and needing to work extra-long hours to get it all done is dangerous for many reasons. Research on the health costs for people working more than fifty-five hours a week is clear. A study published in 2021 by the WHO and ILO concluded that working fifty-five or more hours per week is associated with a higher risk of a stroke and dying from ischemic heart disease, compared with working thirty-five to forty hours.[28]

Other research shows that working long hours is counterproductive. Erin Reid, a professor at Boston University's Questrom School of Business, found that working eighty hours a week does not make a person more productive. In a surprising twist, it was revealed that managers couldn't tell the difference between people who worked the full eighty hours and those who pretended to. The output was the same.[29]

When I thought about Ronnie's unsustainable work hours, I believed another way of thinking about this was not only possible – it was vital. I asked Ronnie what a breakthrough would look like for her, and she laughed and said, 'If I could work sixty hours a week, that would be amazing. But it's not possible.'

I could see why she felt it wasn't possible, but the culture notwithstanding, I believed this was her mindset talking. What was scarce wasn't so much time; it was more surprising. Ronnie was missing a juicier vision for her life that didn't have work in every part of it. I asked Ronnie to imagine what life at seventy hours of work could look like. She dreamed about taking the train to Geneva with her husband on Sundays and visiting museums. They would sit in a café at 8pm a few nights a week and enjoy dinner together.

What might sixty hours look like? Even though it felt like a fantasy, Ronnie got excited about what was emerging. Sixty hours felt visceral! She would cook more often. She would go back to doing Pilates. She and her husband would take their dog on a rambling walk on the weekends.

With four weeks of coaching, Ronnie got her workweek down to seventy hours. She did so by critically examining her unthinking response to saying yes to everything. She noticed how she would step in to fix things her team had done – and then questioned whether this perfectionism and control was warranted. (News flash – it wasn't. Their version was just fine.) She was more rigorous about accepting requests.

Ronnie found newer ways to achieve the same outcome. For instance, one of the time-consuming reports she had to do didn't offer the organisation much value. She streamlined what was needed and displayed the information in ways that made it more accessible. Ronnie became more about what was essential and where her biggest impact lay. She thought strategically instead of reactively. Ronnie had motivation for these changes because her vision for life was pulling her forward. The benefits of her new mindset outweighed the old patterns.

Within three months, Ronnie's working hours stabilised at sixty per week. Something she had believed was impossible became possible. Her performance review showed no drop in productivity, and her team-leading score improved. Ronnie believes that was because she felt less stressed and had more space to support and empower her global team. Her conditions didn't change – she still had work to do, results to produce, deadlines to meet and a team to empower. What changed was her mindset, propelled by a clearer vision for what she wanted her life to look like.

Abundance versus enough

In the grip of scarcity, we lose sight of what we have. We look outside for measures of wealth or success. We look to the share price, our bank account, the number of Instagram followers, the size of our budget, or the hours in a day. The scarcity mindset thrives because we overemphasise these measurements and invalidate the source of our greatest wealth.

So what is the antidote to scarcity? All over the world, when I ask this question, people usually respond with 'abundance'. We just love and want abundance! An abundance of time. Money. Friends. Champagne.

But as author and activist Lynne Twist writes, 'Abundance is merely the flip side of scarcity. You strive to get more than you need because you believe or fear there is not enough.'[30]

I love this perspective. Consider that the pull to abundance is about always having what you want as soon as you want it. It's about having more than you need. Feel the pressure this brings with it. Even squirrels only collect enough acorns for that winter. They don't collect acorns to last fifty years.

The abundance mindset is a trap.

The abundance mindset is a trap. It's like the Buddhist notion of a hungry ghost – always consuming and never satisfied. We think that more of anything/everything is better. More. More. More. We're not safe or accepted or loved until we accumulate more – until we buy more or we are more. The trap is that we can never be ok with what we have now and who we are now. We are always searching for some better, larger, more brilliant version of ourselves. This is unattainable because it is always out of reach.

Lynne Twist writes of this in her classic book, *The Soul Of Money*.[31] 'When you let go of trying to get more of what you don't really need, it frees up oceans of energy to make a difference with what you have.'

What keeps this grasping need for more in place is a deep fear that not only do we not *have* enough – we believe that who we *are* is not enough.

This is why cultivating the mindset of *enough* is a powerful counterpoint to the mindset of scarcity. In doing so, we recognise a radical and uncomfortable truth; that I am enough, and you are enough, and we are enough, as we are. We are enough to lead, live, love, and make our contribution.

We are enough, as we are.

In *Daring Greatly*,[32] Brené Brown calls this mindset of *enough* 'wholehearted living', which means 'engaging in our lives from a place of worthiness. It means cultivating the Courage, Compassion, and Connection to wake up in the morning and think, no matter what gets done and how much is left undone, I am enough.'

The power of being enough recognises that there is nothing fundamentally missing or lacking in who you are. Yes, there are skills to learn and areas to grow – but this does not relate to your essence. Who you are is enough to keep growing, learning and evolving. You don't have to know everything or have everything – and indeed, who would want that?

Our greatest resource

To loosen the grip of the scarcity mindset, it's powerful to notice that our greatest resources do not lie where we think they do. They aren't outside of us, in the number of dollars in a bank account or the years we have left to live.

Our most significant resources lie within us, which is partly why we overlook and undervalue them.

Instead, our most significant resources lie within us, which is partly why we overlook and undervalue them. These resources are bountiful, and we access them when we *lead in*. They include creativity, ingenuity, resourcefulness, go-get-it-ness and boldness. They encompass our compassion, empathy and willingness to work in service of something mighty. And they embody our ability to work with others and to think about our thinking. Tapping into these resources can help us overcome any number of shortages, lack and limitations.

A client was facing wipeout at the start of the pandemic. Their entire business model was in the restaurant and food service business, and lockdowns rendered it obsolete overnight. I had worked with the leadership team on mindsets, so the CEO was aware enough not to go into a default scarcity mindset when conditions changed overnight. Sure, his gut twisted, and he was anxious, but he did not let that determine his response. Instead, he held the space of possibility and pulled the team together to unleash their collective brilliance.

Within two weeks, a new business was created and operationalised. No staff lost their jobs. Profitability only dipped ten per cent, and the new business idea elevated the company once lockdown ended. Diversifying the product offer made them more robust. On paper, this business lost everything at the start of the pandemic – if you ignore its most potent assets and resources – the collective ability and ingenuity of its people.

As this team showed, you can experience scarcity – and yet not lead from a scarcity mindset. That's because your conditions don't determine your mindset – you do.

You can experience scarcity – and yet not lead from a scarcity mindset.

When you're next feeling scarcity, remember you have what it takes to figure it out. Instead of sliding into Victim mindset and triggering hopelessness and fear, try this scenario. Consider that 'yes, I need to take action to work out my financial situation (or whatever I'm feeling scarce about), but I don't need to go into a scarcity mindset. I'm enough as I am. I can unlock the resources within me to navigate this situation and change it.'

This isn't just a theory

Let me share a very personal story.

In my twenties, I got into significant financial difficulty. We'd just had our second child, I wasn't in paid employment, and my husband's business was not going well. Money was so tight that we'd hunt for loose change behind the couch to buy bread and milk. I took out credit cards to manage the debt and juggled between each one, borrowing off one to pay the other. Creditors hounded us, and it was an incredibly stressful time. I was full of shame and embarrassment. 'How had this happened? What was wrong with me?'

I kept it secret as I couldn't be straight with anyone. The cheque was always in the mail. I looked at my peers who all seemed to be doing well, eating out at restaurants, seemingly without a care in the world. This only compounded my shame.

Not understanding mindsets, I didn't differentiate myself from my situation. I personified my scarcity. I believed I was bad with money. That I was poor. In my mind, I needed someone to rescue us as we couldn't do it for ourselves. I felt hopeless. I could not see a way out other than winning the lottery.

One morning I experienced a moment of grace. I remember walking from my lounge room to the kitchen and suddenly realised that my life was being held hostage to fear over money! It was a flash of radical clarity. In that instance, I observed my thinking and my life from outside the scarcity bubble and saw how worry consumed every moment. My life wasn't my own. The big realisation was that yes, I owed the bank thousands of dollars, and yes, I was in a financial hole – yet this was not who I was.

When I recognised this, I laughed! I could see the mindset so clearly – what I'd made my situation mean about me and how ludicrously disempowering that was. I had been beating myself up every waking moment. I would quake when the phone rang as I knew it would be another pissed off creditor. My entire life had been hijacked – and I had let it happen.

It took a couple of years to reverse the situation, but we did. For a start, my conversations with creditors changed. Not long after my moment of grace, Carol rang from the bank. She was my nemesis, and I dreaded her calls. We were in a dance of doom: she wanted money from me, and I would give her a date when she would get it, that we both knew I couldn't keep.

This day was different. I welcomed her call and apologised for not being consistently upfront with her. I told her that although I owed the bank money, I had never done her any harm and would appreciate her speaking to me respectfully. She heard me and accepted. We laid out a plan that took a couple of years to pay off, but I did, and in Carol, I had a real partner.

In changing my scarcity mindset, debts didn't magically disappear. Yet centring myself in being enough was the start of the road out of financial tyranny. It's amazing the different choices and actions I took when this mindset changed – ones I could not have imagined when mired in fear and scarcity. I was not doomed to impotently and passively carry forward my parent's story of poverty and loss. I could figure it out. And I did.

Using the Mindset Process to unlock a scarcity mindset

It's your turn now to use the Mindset Process to get unhooked from your scarcity mindset. What do you feel you are lacking? (Ok, just choose one to start!)

Step one: Notice

Firstly, *notice* the mindset. What am I saying, feeling and believing about this situation? What thoughts am I running (or are running me?). As I shared in my story, noticing this was the first step to getting out of my financial troubles. Bring your attention to the feelings that come with what you believe. Acknowledge the shame (if it's there), or the inadequacy, or loss – whatever you feel.

You don't need to fix or change it, just observe. In doing so, you might even feel it soften. Too often, we downplay or ignore our feelings around scarcity and try to bury them. But they are often our most primal and deeply felt. They can go back to childhood, even when you were pre-verbal. The feeling of not having enough support, or care, or love cuts deep and can be triggered even by surface-level scarcity. Notice this and give it some space.

Too often, we downplay or ignore our feelings around scarcity and try to bury them.

What scarcity thinking are you noticing? Perhaps it's a lack of hope when you consider the future of our planet? Notice what you're thinking and saying about it. It might be 'We've run out of time to turn it around.' 'There isn't enough political will to make the changes we need.' 'I don't have any hope that I can do anything.' Feel the feelings that come with this.

Maybe you feel pressure at work and worry you won't make a deadline. What do you believe about this? Is it 'We don't have time? We don't have the right people?' In noticing, you might find something else is going on. Maybe what's really there for you is a lack of respect. A belief that you are taken for granted. Keep noticing what's going on for you.

If you feel a scarcity of confidence to ask someone out, notice what you say and make it mean. 'It probably won't last past one date.' 'I'm not interesting enough.' 'I'm not the type of person that others find attractive.' What is coming up for you? Is it hopelessness? Anger? Sadness? What's the scarcity really about? Keep noticing.

Wherever you are stuck and feel scarcity, observe the feelings and thoughts that arise. Is your heart rate elevated? Are you feeling warm? Are you getting tense and angry? Whatever it is, that's fine. Just notice it.

Good. You're doing great.

Remember to notice the link between what you are thinking and feeling and the meaning or reason you're attaching to it.

Some examples might be

- I want to buy a house, but *my ex took all my money.*

- I want to go dancing, but *I don't have anyone to go with me.*

- I want to raise money for my friend's cancer treatment, but *people I know don't have money to give.*

You can see the scarcity mindset in the italics. It's the reason or the blocker preventing you from achieving your aim. Each excuse is based on lack, and each makes complete sense.

Step two: Question

As you know, the next part of the process is to *question* the mindset. Is it true that the team doesn't have time? Is it true I have no confidence? (Like none?) Is it true your ex has all your money? Now the answer may be yes, it is true, or no, it's not true. Your budget may well have been slashed by twenty-five per cent. And your ex may have been awarded a large financial settlement. The purpose of questioning is not to fight with reality but to unhook it from the meaning you give it.

The purpose of questioning is not to fight with reality but to unhook it from the meaning you give it.

If your budget has been cut by twenty-five per cent, does that mean you can't deliver the scope? How might you rethink this? What could you drop from the work while still providing the guts of what the department needs? How can you reconfigure this? What conversation is required to get additional resources? How do you support the team to focus on the task and not the loss? What opportunity is there in this? What new way of thinking can be unlocked?

If your financial situation has taken a hit because of a settlement to an ex-spouse or another reason, does that mean you can't buy a home? You might not (yet) be able to afford the manor of your dreams, but what can you afford? How can you refigure your finances? What else is possible?

To move out of a scarcity mindset, you must remove your attachment to the story, and questioning helps with that – especially around money. Let go of justifications for why you don't have what you believe you should have. Explore the many other ways to get what you want by viewing your resources differently.

Some years ago, Steve and I wanted to buy a home in the area we had moved to in northern New South Wales, but we couldn't afford it. I was working for The Hunger Project on a small non-profit salary, and Steve had started a new business that was going well but not yet providing reliable income to borrow against.

Instead of succumbing to a 'poor us' scarcity mindset, we looked at what resources we had. These included wonderful friends and our excellent reputations as people of integrity. We approached another couple who were also interested in buying in the area, and together we bought twenty-two hectares in the rainforest. There were two, run-down dwellings on the land, one of which was an old banana packing shed. Over time we have made them into lovely homes. We achieved our goal by thinking through what we did have rather than focusing on what we lacked.

Other common scarcity traps

Love: *I want to find love, but there's no one out there for me.* Is it true that on a planet of seven billion people, there is not someone for you? How do you benefit from this belief? If you gave up the idea that 'there's no one out there for me', what might you do?

Confidence: *I don't have confidence.* Get curious. Is it true that 'I'm not confident?' What does confidence even mean? Is it a feeling? Do you need to feel confident before you take action? If you were confident, what action would you take? How is not feeling confident working for you?'

Business success: *I don't have enough sales for my business to succeed.* What non-material assets can you draw upon? Who can help you make a plan for your rebound?' How can you nurture yourself to fill the empty well caused by stress? What new business opening can you fill that's not met in your market?

Keep asking questions to get under your thinking.

Steps three and four

You've *noticed* your scarcity mindset, and you've *questioned* it. Now it's time to *choose.* What would be the most empowering mindset for you now? When caught in financial woes in my twenties, it was '*I can do this. I can find a way.*' If your circumstances have suddenly changed – maybe the deadline for an initiative has been brought forward – instead of complaining, choose a mindset. It might be simply '*I've got this. I have what I need to figure this out.*'

Speaking of which, I love Marie Forleo's motto (and now book title) that 'Everything is figureoutable'.[33] This is a fantastic mindset to choose.

One of the most simple yet profound mindsets to choose is this: 'I am enough.'

One of the most simple yet profound mindsets to choose is this: 'I am enough.'

Lastly, take an *action* to accompany your new mindset. Make this an action step that someone with this new mindset would take. It might be to speak with one creditor. It might be to bring your team together and ideate a new way forward that uses the limitations instead of being tyrannised by them. Make your action small and doable. See what happens. Then take the next step. Keep walking around in this new mindset, knowing it will feel strange and uncomfortable at first. It's displacing your old thinking and actions, so give it time to find its groove.

From little things, big things grow

Some of the most significant scarcity mindset transformations have been from people living in true deprivation. Women and men I met across Africa and South Asia face real shortages of almost everything essential – food, water, income, land. They have every reason to be always laid low by the sheer enormity of what they lack. And this would never change if our greatest resource lay outside us. As we shall see, even in the harshest of conditions, a scarcity mindset can be overcome through liberating resources that are often overlooked – your potential and the support of others.

In my first book, *Unlikely Leaders*, I told the story of Rheeana, who, as a young woman, had little standing in her village in rural Bangladesh.

I first met her twenty years ago at a small meeting, in a tiny tin shed, on a hot day. Women (with children and chickens) crowded together, sharing the challenges they faced. It was hot, sweaty and noisy. Rheeana stood up and began to talk about her life before being trained by The Hunger Project. She shared feeling hopeless about the poverty in her life and her village. She had believed nothing would ever change as she couldn't read or write, and she was poor. What hope was there for someone like her? The very idea that there might be another way was not even worth considering. That was for other people in other lands. Not for her.

The mindset work Rheeana did with The Hunger Project opened a window to new possibilities for how she could improve her life. One of these involved working collectively with other women. Rheeana joined such a group, and together they pooled their resources – in this case, solidarity and rice. In a community where people often ate only one bowl of rice a day with a few fried chillies on top, the women made a profound investment in their future. Every day, they set aside a fistful of dry rice to contribute as a kitty to the group. Each week, they converted that rice to cash at the market and gave the pooled money to a different woman to help start her business. And one week, that woman was Rheeana.

Becoming economically empowered changed everything. Rheeana started small, with just a few chickens and grew from there. Each step along the way built her confidence. The strength of her ties with the other women and her conviction about what she believed her village deserved became her biggest resource. The following year Rheeana intervened to stop a child marriage – an action that would have been unimaginable earlier.

Years after first meeting this shy woman in that crowded tin shack, Rheeana and I met for tea in her small house. We sipped our hot drinks together and talked about what had happened in the intervening years. I showed her the photo I took of her as a young woman, and we both smiled at how we once were.

I looked around at the lovely home she had created. Hand-stitched linen covered the table, and chickens clucked on the ground below. Rheeana was now managing her household, had enough food, and was literate. What was even more remarkable to me was her sharing, almost as an aside, that she had prevented more than thirty-five child marriages over the past twenty years. I could see what a huge resource this quiet, courageous woman is to her community.

Rheeana's story shows that a scarcity mindset and believing that conditions determine your life, can change. She grew up in poverty and lack, yet powerful resources were there, only hidden from view. These resources – unlocking her mindset through leadership training; support from other women; using what she had even though it wasn't much (a fistful of rice); and creating a vision for her future – liberated her from hunger. These overlooked and undervalued assets were her true source of wealth.

She grew up in poverty and lack, yet powerful resources were there, only hidden from view.

Rheeana demonstrates for all of us that even the most entrenched and justified scarcity can be overcome by harnessing the power of mindset.

Key points

- Scarcity is a universal limiting mindset that feels personal but affects most people.

- Scarcity is neither your birthright nor your fate. Your biggest resource lies within. It's in your ability to collaborate, think about your thinking, work with others, and choose your mindset.

- Be wary of wanting abundance as your measure of success. Focusing on having too much can mean you are emphasising the wrong thing. It may mean you are still caught up in scarcity and not free to focus on what truly matters.

- Owning that you are enough as you are, is a radical and liberating choice. It means that you are worthy and deserving of leading, making an impact and living the life you want. While there are always things to learn, you are enough.

Questions to consider

- If I believed I was truly enough, how would that feel?

- If I believed I was enough, what would I do now?

- What are my greatest resources?

- What would an inventory of my inner assets look like?

- How might I think about my resources more expansively?

Eight

Introducing the Mindset Process to Others

Spread the mindset message

When I work with leaders, one of the first things they ask is how to use the Mindset Process with their team members. It's often because there's a problem with someone or something – 'Kelly in Accounts really needs this!' Or maybe their partner at home. Or their kids!

That may be so, but it's essential to gain mindset experience yourself before you go there. I can't say this strongly enough. Make sure you are *leading in* before coaching others. Keep bringing awareness and choice to how you show up by catching your own assumptions and default leadership styles. As leaders, we must put ourselves in the arena before encouraging others to step in.

There are two reasons for this. First, you will have no credibility guiding someone else if you are not authentic about your own mindsets. If you are constantly reacting unfavourably to market changes, clients or your own emotions, you are leading out, and coaching others to *lead in* will fall flat. (No one likes being preached to by a hypocrite.) Second, putting in the effort demonstrates that working with mindsets isn't a 'been there, done that' proposition. The work is ongoing because we all have triggers that trip us into behaving less than we would like. Being a student of the Mindset Process honours this in an open and non-judgemental way.

So before helping others with their mindset, be honest about how you are showing up. Are you reactive? Are you flaring up in staff meetings? Are you turning into a Dictator when Kelly from Accounts is being annoying? Do you want to *do* the Mindset Process *to* someone? Do you think your team needs fixing?

The hard truth about leading is that first, you must lead yourself.

You won't be the first to answer yes to any of these. So it's good to *notice* your motivations. (See how this works?) The hard truth about leading is that first, you must lead yourself – that's why this book is called *Lead In*. As the pilot tells us, we must fit our own oxygen masks first. As leaders, we must bring awareness and honesty to the way we show up. If a fixed or limited mindset is running you, and you are not open with yourself about this, you are not ready to introduce the Mindset Process to someone else. It just won't work.

Once you understand your mindsets and see this as a great tool, then do share with others. I'm not saying to wait until you're perfect (that is not possible) or 'really good' at mindsets. No. Just make sure you, too, are on the mat as you guide others. When you are *leading in* it becomes natural to want to share this with people.

If you are ready to share the Mindset Process with others in your life or your team, here are some dos and donts. I'm starting with the don'ts because there are a few key things to be aware of first.

Don't

Don't just tell people 'that's a fixed mindset' when they are struggling – even if you clearly hear that it is. One leadership team I worked with was so excited about the edge mindsets gave them that they wanted to get their direct reports onto it. They'd tell me 'Ben has a really fixed mindset'. You will likely notice when team members have a scarcity mindset or a belief that keeps them stuck, but don't just tell them. Such announcements are counterproductive without context.

Don't use what you know to belittle another person. Even if they show a limited mindset – how is it helpful if you randomly point that out as if it is their personal failing? People feel judged, confused and labelled when terms are thrown around.

Speaking of which, don't judge the person you want to empower. If you are frustrated or have given up on them, they will pick it up straight away. Vulnerability is essential for the Mindset Process to work. When criticised, flight, fright or fight can be triggered – none of which are conducive to being open to learning something new.

Don't make people wrong because they are displaying a limited mindset. Don't use this to box people into an identity that becomes a truth; 'Oh, Jamie is just so negative about our projected outlook. He really needs a different mindset.' In doing so, you ironically fall into a fixed mindset yourself about him. When you make someone wrong, you are, by default, making yourself right. So, would you rather be right or get curious and empower a team member? And you might even realise that someone's attitude is not a limited mindset at all.

When you make someone wrong, you are, by default, making yourself right. So, would you rather be right or get curious and empower a team member?

The leaders of a large regional not-for-profit organisation were working on their strategy. The executive director was incredibly proud of it as he spent a lot of late nights and concentrated thinking to make it as good as possible. When working with the centre managers, he was annoyed at his colleague Michelle's negativity. In our mentoring session, he asked, 'Why isn't she on board? She's disruptive and questions everything. There's no need for her to make it so difficult. I just want everyone to get on board so we can go out and do this!' He put it down to Michelle's limited mindset, 'she just doesn't get it'. The ED hadn't considered that Michelle's mindset might not be the issue.

In this case, Michelle might be speaking her truth about the flaws in the strategy, in order to make it more robust. When you are attached to people agreeing with you or with the strategy you have authored, it's easy to dismiss counter comments as another person's Mindset when, in fact, the mindset limitations could be on your side!

Don't blunder in without doing the work on yourself first. If you see an incident where you think mindsets are holding someone back, use the Mindset Process on your relationship before speaking to them. It need only take a moment. Notice how they show up for you. Observe when you feel triggered or annoyed or want to rush in and be a hero. Question it. Do you want to rescue them? Do you want to solve their problems? Do you think that will fix them? Does this handle a problem for you? The work is still with you if you answer 'yes' to any of those questions.

You've noticed and questioned. Now choose how you want to show up for them. Put your default mindset to one side and be with them in service and love. Whether they're a child, teenager or adult, centre yourself in their innate ability. Widen your perspective so the current block isn't all you can see about them. Then take action based on that. Have a fruitful conversation. Bring the team together in a way that makes a difference. Show care and concern instead of irritation and annoyance.

Show care and concern instead of irritation and annoyance.

Do

Do expect this to be more than a one-off. You can't just do a seminar on mindsets with your team and then expect them to start using the Mindset

Process like pros. Understanding mindsets is one thing. Practically applying these concepts takes rigour, courage and application. Think of it like a craft that takes time and practice to create a thing of beauty. So too, with this. Expect initial attempts to be clumsy or lacklustre.

Do share why working with mindsets is essential and the difference it makes to your leadership abilities. Give an example. Don't talk in theory. Be open and honest about the shift in how you view your leadership or the value of the team – share what you've learned about yourself.

Andy is an executive at a national education company, and he put it this way: 'I called my team together. They'd been hearing me talk about mindsets for a while, but they had no real idea of what that meant. Instead of launching in, I followed Cathy's advice and started with my personal journey. I said, "I've noticed how I don't really listen – even when I think I do. When you come to me, I say 'yeah' and nod my head, but I'm not hearing you. I'm thinking instead of how I'm going to have to fix this."'

Sharing further, Andy said: 'I learned that this was a limiting mindset I had which was "here we go again, I'll have to sort this out!". This meant I didn't really listen to you, and I didn't empower you to grow and solve things yourself. You are all so capable, but I just wasn't letting that shine through.' Andy's team was floored. In this simple act of sharing, they saw the power of overcoming limiting mindsets in action. He wasn't preaching or trying to fix them. He used his own example to open up new possibilities for his team.

Do give people space to figure it out their own way. What might appear an easy mindset fix may have layers for the stuck person. Jo discovered this when working with one of her reports. Karl was a new hire into her finance team and had some customer-facing aspects to his role. When sitting in on his client meetings, Jo noticed how much Karl talked over and interrupted the customer. She spoke to him about this behaviour and found he was unaware of it. They discussed what mindset he wanted to choose before going to his next meetings, including being curious, in service and attentive. Karl endeavoured to practice this. Yet Jo kept getting feedback about how off-putting Karl still was.

Jo knew she needed to check her own mindset first as she was frustrated and annoyed. 'How come Karl is still messing this up? I've told him what's not working. We've spoken about his mindset.' Jo knew going into a discussion this way might feel justified to her, but it was not how she wanted to be as a leader who empowered her team. So she got herself into a coaching mindset.

In their subsequent conversation, Karl had an epiphany. He realised that he felt he needed to show he knew his stuff in customer meetings because he didn't want them to think they were getting lesser service because he was young and new to the team.

A thought visibly struck Karl. 'I used to feel this way when I had to change school a few times. I sort of barrelled past the embarrassment of being the new kid. I didn't ever let myself just settle in. That's what speaking to customers has felt like.' In noticing this, Karl acknowledged to himself that this might have worked as a coping strategy as a kid, but as an adult, he could choose a new way to be with people in unfamiliar circumstances where something was at stake. That helped his new behaviours stick.

Do share that mindset work is backed by rigorous research and considered by many to be the most powerful tool you can have in your leadership toolkit. Give some examples – they might be from this book or your ongoing reading.

Do come with an open heart. Notice when you feel judgemental and choose to put it to one side.

Do come with an open heart.

Tips and examples

Reward actions, not personality traits

Even star players lose their edge and brilliance when praised only for their nature or results. Categorising someone in this way locks them into past performance, and over time reduces the runway they have to branch out and try a different approach. In today's world, such a mindset will dull the performance of even the most accomplished person.

Let's say one of your team members achieves a win, and you celebrate this by saying 'You're a star'. It might feel nice in the moment but doesn't help them *lead in*. It cements a belief there is something 'natural' or innate about what they've done, and it diminishes or invisibilises the effort and development it took to achieve the result. Having praise be about one's identity makes it hard to distinguish what worked from who they are, and it can pile the pressure on. When eventually they don't succeed, they have no other reference or framework other than they must have lost their edge.

Instead, focus on what was done, and how it was done, and celebrate that.

Instead, focus on what was done, and how it was done, and celebrate that.

Using mindsets to support people's growth works both in and out of the office. For example, if your child achieves a great result in an art project, the response to help develop a growth mindset could be, 'Awesome, what a result! I know you put a lot of effort into the design, and you really figured out the best way to capture it,' instead of, 'Awesome, what a result! You're so talented at art.'

Model the mindset

When you hear people repeatedly complain about the same thing, there is likely a mindset at play. So what do you do if a team member keeps complaining about how busy they are or how unreasonable a particular client is?

You model the mindset change you hope to encourage. You bring curiosity, compassion and openness to the discussion.

Anita's colleague, Alberto, felt resentful and overwhelmed by all he had to do. He constantly vented about this to Anita, and while she had some sympathy, she didn't think his attitude was helping himself or the team. Anita was empathetic and practical in addressing this, and she recreated her conversation as follows:

'Yeah, Alberto, it sucks about the amount of work on and the time to do it, especially with the shipping delays we've been having, but I notice that this is really eating away at you, and I don't think that's good for you or the team. There are definitely aspects of this situation you can't control, but let's look at what you can. How else can you think about this? What can you do to relieve the overwhelm? Let's map that out together.'

You can see in this example how Anita was straight and helpful. She acknowledged where he was at and offered another perspective. She didn't lecture him or make him wrong.

Be explicit with your team

If you want to gain momentum and alignment around mindsets with your team, be upfront about it. Help people understand mindsets and create an open space to identify those that hold them back. (It's one reason why organisations ask me to run *Lead In* programs with them.) Let your people know you expect them to work on their mindsets and that doing so is integral to the organisation's success. That is why modelling the Leader's mindset is so important.

Talk to them about being a *lead in* leader. Walk your people through the Mindset Process and show them the infinity model in Chapter Six. Share what *Notice* is, and work with them individually and as a group to notice which mindsets hold them back. Help them to *Question* and encourage the sort of unattached exploration that facilitates change. Invite them to *Choose* a new mindset and help them see how this might look in action. Then have them determine what *Action* steps they will take to embody the new mindset muscle.

Check your language

The way we speak about things holds enormous power over how we view what's happening. Language does give rise to reality – given that reality is so open to interpretation. The world does what it does, and we attach meaning to it through our words and thoughts. How you speak about something or someone matters.

Language does give rise to reality – given that reality is so open to interpretation.

When you internally berate yourself, you underscore a belief that you are not good enough. You might notice thoughts along the line of, 'I shouldn't have done that. Why am I so stupid? I can't do that' or other unhelpful statements. These have the power to shape your world if thought often enough. Notice what you are saying. Question it. (One of my favourite ways to short circuit my negative internal dialogue is to ask, 'Is this the most empowering thing to think? What is a more loving way I can look at this?') Choose a new mindset or a new way to interpret your situation, and start to live it.

An oldie (and a goodie) is to add 'yet' to a statement about something you can't do. It opens up the possibility for progress through improvement.

Cary had been learning Indonesian for a few months and was frustrated that he couldn't hold a conversation the way he wanted. Instead of saying 'I can't speak Indonesian' – and therefore give up – he tweaked it to 'I can't speak Indonesian, yet'. This little addition kept his hope alive that he would get there with more practice.

Keep the bigger picture in mind

Keeping the overall goal in your sights smooths out bumps and roadblocks when something important is at stake. It's easy to trip into a limited mindset and feel defeated. Many great initiatives stall when we allow difficult conditions to dictate our momentum and resolve. While this is understandable, recentring the bigger picture is an excellent way to overcome this mindset.

Anything worth doing is full of difficulties, and it's naïve to expect otherwise.

If your team is struggling with an initiative, and this is exacerbating a fixed mindset of 'we can't do this' or a limited one of 'this is just not possible', reconnect them to the vision. Remind them why the project is important. Share that stumbles are normal and should be expected. The ball doesn't always bounce in your direction. The way forward isn't clear, but that's not a bad thing. Reframe 'something's wrong' into a 'shit happens' mindset and create a more mature and robust relationship with obstacles. Anything worth doing is full of difficulties, and it's naïve to expect otherwise. Use the bigger picture of what you are about as your north star.

Use questions to shift perspective

It's easy to be hijacked into an unhelpful mindset at any time. It could be a team member's comment, pushback from a client, feeling time pressure, losing a customer, or a political announcement you don't agree with. When you find yourself in a complex or difficult situation, notice which path you are heading down. Are you leading in – or out? Are you responding – or reacting? Are you choosing a Leader's mindset – or do you find yourself complaining, looking for who is at fault and what's wrong?

Are you leading in - or out?

Marilee Adams' classic book *Change Your Questions, Change Your Life*,[34] talks about how particular questions can help someone heading down a path of negative thinking to recalibrate. Her Choice Map is an excellent illustration of how one can move from what she calls the 'judger' path onto the 'learner' path through a series of questions.

Adapting her work, I find the following questions useful to help people *lead in*.

When the team is stuck, frustrated or disempowered, a leader's overarching question is: How can I shift perspective so they are empowered?

To encourage your team to *lead in*, try some of these:

- Is what we're saying about this situation true?

- How else can we think about this?

- What assumptions are we making?

- What new ways can we try?

- Given this, now what's possible?

- What can we do differently?

- Who do we need to be as a team to have this work?

- What can we learn (from this situation, this failure, this obstacle)?

- What's missing?

When individual team members come from a limited mindset, a leader's overarching question is: How can I help them grow?

To encourage an individual to *lead in*, try some of these:

- What happened? (As in, what actually happened, not the story around it.)

- What are you seeing, thinking or feeling right now?

- What are you making this mean?

- Is this interpretation true?

- How else might you think about this?

- What do you need to say or do to make this right?

- What action can you take right now that would make a difference?

Key points

- Make sure you keep developing your own Leader's mindset. Bring awareness to your motivations, criticisms and assumptions before helping others.

- If you want to guide someone into a new possibility, approach your conversation open-heartedly and without judgement.

- Don't make it about you. The onus and agency are always with the person who wants to move past their limiting beliefs and stuck patterns.

- Remember that you can never do this for someone else. You're not trying to fix them. All you can do is encourage and hold a clear space for people to grow and develop.

Questions to consider

- What could be possible if my whole organisation were Leading In?

- How can I encourage a Leader's mindset in my team?

- How can I keep my own mindset practice front and centre?

- How can I empower others to think expansively?

Afterword

To *lead in* at this time is to accept the power you have to make a difference. This is available to everyone, but few know how to unlock it – or even if they should. Too much human potential has been lost or locked out, and this must change. Now is the time for good people to rise to the demands of leadership and have a say in the future.

My intention in writing *Lead In* has been to equip you with the tools and examples to do just that. I have wanted to demystify the process of effective leadership, and make it available, no matter who you are and where you live. Mindsets are one of the most profound – and accessible – tools we have. I hope this book provided you with what you need to lead the profound and meaningful changes you are called to make – in your life, your work and your world.

Working with mindsets can seem clunky at first, and that's ok. It's a bit like learning to drive in a manual car and focusing on all the things you need to do: check rear vision mirror, handbrake off, foot on brake, turn on engine, foot on clutch, foot on accelerator at the same pace as taking foot off clutch – I mean – it's a lot! I remember when I got my manual licence and drove down the street for the first time. I couldn't believe people did all this while talking and listening to the radio!

I have wanted to demystify the process of effective leadership, and make it available, no matter who you are and where you live.

Using the Mindset Process can feel a bit like that at first. When faced with an obstacle, start with Noticing. Observe what you think and feel and what you are making this mean. Then Question that – is it even true? What's another way I can think about this? Now Choose a new mindset that expands your leadership and your space for freedom and joy. And then take Action in the world, stepping forward with this new mindset. With your new awareness, you'll discover other beliefs that get in your way, and so you begin the process again. Over time and with practice, you'll find the bumps even out, and the path widens and gets smoother.

That is why the Mindset Process is designed as an infinity loop. Leaders who *lead in* know this is a journey. There is no final destination, only continual growth and evolution. They are as present as possible to the motivations and beliefs that hold them back.

Bringing awareness to our thoughts, beliefs and motivations is like an onion. As our ability to achieve and succeed grows, we face different limitations and new challenges. Accepting this is key to *leading in*.

Expect it. The human pull to evolve means we will always brush up against how we've changed and what is now possible.

Having read this book and seen through some of your mindset blockers, you'll realise that you can choose how to show up every day. You'll start to notice a rhythm. You'll catch yourself in your old habits and fixed mindsets. You'll notice when you are reacting to the conditions instead of determining who you'll be and how you'll respond to those conditions. When you start to fume about something, you'll stop and look at it in a new light. What can you do about this problem? Is this something you want to give your energy to? How do you choose to be around this?

You might even find yourself looking for new friends because it will be hard to spend hours with people who bitch and moan for their recreation. You might find yourself drawn to interesting people, working on cool solutions for an issue you care about, and you may join them to add your shoulder to the wheel. This has certainly happened to me, and I grew because of it.

Having this awareness can be annoying at first because now you see all those tips and tricks that got you off the hook for what they are. You will still have scarcity mindset moments – but you'll know what's happening. You can choose to succumb for a bit (who doesn't like a whinge every now and then?), but this lower level leadership becomes less attractive over time.

Committing to being a *lead in* leader gives you tremendous power to shape your life and your world. When you own what you want and what matters most, you won't let prevailing conditions or old stories of your inexperience, failures or lack of confidence get in the way.

You can extend this to your work: what could be possible in your organisation if you empowered others to *lead in*? If your department had many people choosing a Leader's mindset, what could you accomplish that currently is beyond you? How much more effective would you be? What extra space would you have for great work if fewer Dictators, Victims and Delayers were on display?

Bold, courageous, effective and heart-centred leadership is available to all. Mindsets are a valuable and powerful tool to catalyse innovation and breakthroughs in response to challenges. Whether you work in a village field or a city skyscraper, we all have work to do. Let's create thoughtful and aware leadership. Let's empower people to *lead in*. In doing so, we expand the team of dedicated, committed, and courageous people who can work alongside us for a better future.

Work with Cathy

Cathy Burke supports organisations and people around the world to lead courageously and effectively, no matter the challenges and conditions. She is known for unlocking capability, possibility, and leadership and she does this with clarity, grace and deep humanity.

There are a number of ways you can work with Cathy:

Leadership training

Cathy's *Lead In* programs empower teams and companies to develop mindset and leadership abilities to expand their power to lead effectively.

She also offers specific transformational trainings for women to *lead in*, based on her decades of experience working with women across many complex settings.

Lead In programs are also highly recommended for NextGen leaders.

Mentor

Often professionals need individual support to grow to the next level. Cathy mentors ambitious, heart-centred people who want to expand their impact and do so in a way that gives them space to reflect and recalibrate. She is a trusted, wise head for leaders who have big dreams and a lot going on.

Speaker

Cathy is an experienced public speaker, delivering warm and engaging keynotes globally. She has spoken in front of audiences of 11,000 people, as well as intimate fireside chats at leadership summits. Cathy lives her message and imparts this to her audiences in ways that make her a popular and in-demand speaker. She leaves people inspired and equipped with new insights to take action in their life.

If you are interested to learn more about how to work with Cathy, please email hello@cathyburke.com.

You can also join Cathy's community!
Each week Cathy shares the latest ideas and thinking on how to lead, live and work differently. It's free.

Use this QR code to join.

About the Author

Cathy Burke helps organisations and people develop the mindsets, leadership and skills needed to address 21st century challenges.

For twenty years, Cathy was CEO for The Hunger Project Australia, and then global vice president, working to end hunger across South Asia and Africa. Cathy was an integral member of a visionary team who developed leadership at scale in villages all over the world. Through this work, millions of the world's poorest people stepped into their leadership and were able to feed themselves and their families.

Cathy now works with executives, teams and dynamic individuals to develop the capabilities and heart needed for a better future. She believes leadership potential is available to everyone and that it has never been more important to activate this in organisations and communities worldwide.

As a leadership trainer, Cathy designs and leads transformational programs. She empowers people's innate capacity to address difficult circumstances and rise to the challenge.

She is a trusted mentor to purpose-driven executives and leaders and a sought-after conference speaker.

Cathy's clients include Commonwealth Bank, eBay, PwC, ANZ Bank and Amazon.

Cathy is a winner of the AFR Top 100 Women of Influence award and the Australian Davos leadership award. She is the author of *Unlikely Leaders: Lessons in Leadership from the Village Classroom (2015)*.

Cathy is married with two children and a rescue dog. She lives on eighty-five acres in the sub-tropical rainforest of northern New South Wales, on the unceded lands of the Widjabul Wia-bal people of Bundjalung nation. In her spare time, she can be found eating mangoes, dancing in her loungeroom, and swimming in the local creek.

More about Cathy can be found at www.cathyburke.com.

You can also connect with her on Linkedin and Instagram.

References

1. The Hunger Project, [Accessed October 2021], https://thp.org/

2. The United Nations Fourth World Conference on Women, Platform for Action, A:47, 1995, Available at: https://www.un.org/womenwatch/daw/beijing/platform/plat1.htm

3. Remarks at the announcement for the Africa Prize for Leadership, Ouagadougou, Burkina Faso, 15 July 1993

4. Brené Brown, *Dare to Lead: Brave Work. Tough Conversations. Whole Hearts*, (New York: Random House, 2018).

5. Stephen R. Covey, *The 7 Habits of Highly Effective People*, (New York: Simon & Schuster, 1990).

6. https://sdgs.un.org/goals

7. Carol Dweck, *Mindset: The New Psychology of Success*, (New York: Ballantine Books, 2006). Further citations of this work are throughout the book.

8. First Five Years, *Why children's mindset matters*. Available at: https://www.firstfiveyears.org.au/child-development/why-childrens-mindset-matters [Accessed July 2021].

9. Carol Dweck, *Mindset*.

10. Carol Dweck, *Mindset*.

11. Satya Nadella, Greg Shaw, Jill Tracie Nichols, and Bill Gates, *Hit Refresh: The Quest to Rediscover Microsoft's Soul and Imagine a Better Future for Everyone*, (HarperCollins: London, 2017).

12. Herminia Ibarra and Aneeta Rattan, Microsoft: instilling a growth mindset. *London Business School Review*, Issue 3 (2018): 50-53.

13. ABC, *Conversations with Richard Fidler, Sarah Kanowski*, [Accessed 2021] https://www.abc.net.au/radio/programs/conversations/ben-crowe/13425314

14. Carol Dweck, *Mindset*.

15. Michelle P. King, *The Fix: How to Overcome the Invisible Barriers That Are Holding Women Back At Work*, (New York: Simon and Schuster, 2020).

16. Adam Grant, *Think Again*, (New York: WH Allen, 2021).

17. Alexandra Appolonia, How BlackBerry went from controlling the smartphone market to a phone of the past, *Business Insider Australia*, 22 November 2019, [Accessed October 2021] https://www.businessinsider.com.au/blackberry-smartphone-rise-fall-mobile-failure-innovate-2019-11?r=US&IR=T

18. Robert Swan, [Accessed October 2021] https://robertswan.com/

19. Katty Kay and Claire Shipman, *The Confidence Code: The Science and Art of Self-Assurance*, (New York: Harper Business, 2014).

20. William Hutchison Murray, *The Scottish Himalayan Expedition*, (London: J.M. Dent & Sons, 1951).

21. T.S. Eliot, *Little Gidding*, (London: Faber and Faber, 1944).

22. Viktor E. Frankl, *Man's Search for Meaning*, (New York: Random House, 2019).

23. Greg McKeown, *Essentialism: The Disciplined Pursuit of Less*, (London: Virgin Books, 2021).

24. Teresa Amabile, and Steven Kramer, *The Progress Principle: Using Small Wins to Ignite Joy, Engagement, and Creativity at Work*, (Boston: Harvard Business Review Press, 2011).

25. Steven Pressfield, *The War of Art: Break Through the Blocks and Win Your Inner Creative Battles*, (New York: Rugged Land, 2002).

26. James Suzman, *Work: A History of How We Spend Our Time*, (London: Bloomsbury Press, 2021).

27. Daniel Kahneman, and Amos Tversky, Advances in Prospect Theory: Cumulative Representation of Uncertainty. *Journal of Risk and Uncertainty*, 5(4), 1992, pp 297-323.

28. Frank Pega, Balint Náfrádi et al, Global, regional, and national burdens of ischemic heart disease and stroke attributable to exposure to long working hours for 194 countries, 2000–2016: A systematic analysis from the WHO/ILO Joint Estimates of the Work-related Burden of Disease and Injury. *Science Direct*. Available at https://www.sciencedirect.com/science/article/pii/S0160412021002208 /

29. Erin Reid, Why Some Men Pretend to Work 80-Hour Weeks, 28 April 2015, [Accessed 2021] https://hbr.org/2015/04/why-some-men-pretend-to-work-80-hour-weeks

30. Lynne Twist, Sufficiency is Not Abundance, [Accessed 2021] https://www.awakin.org/read/view.php?tid=2097

31. Lynne Twist, *The Soul of Money: Transforming Your Relationship with Money and Life*, (New York: W.W. Norton and Company, 2017).

32. Brené Brown, *Daring Greatly: How the Courage to be Vulnerable Transforms the Way We Live, Love, Parent, and Lead*, (London: Penguin Books, 2016).

33. Marie Forleo, *Everything is Figureoutable*, (New York: Penguin Publishing Group, 2021).

34. Marilee G. Adams, *Change Your Questions, Change Your Life: 10 Powerful Tools For Life And Work*, (2nd Ed. San Francisco: Berrett-Koehler Publishers, 2009).

CPSIA information can be obtained
at www.ICGtesting.com
Printed in the USA
BVHW030324150422
634018BV00002B/13